"St. Paul said that by baptism, 'all are given to drink of the same Spirit.' However, the Catholic community is still learning how to engage the gifts of all its people as potential leaders in the mission of the church to the world. Combining a rich background in leadership with his own deep Catholic faith, Chris Lowney offers a clarion call and a way forward to create faith communities where 'everyone leads.' This will be an invaluable contribution to forging a church for the twenty-first century."
**—Thomas Groome, Boston College; director of The Church in the 21st Century Center**

"Chris Lowney has applied his extensive business background and made an important contribution to the ongoing discussions about the future of the Catholic church, not just in the United States, but worldwide. He not only accurately describes the current crisis that the church faces, but his EASTeR solution is both workable and consistent with church teachings and values. But this book goes beyond merely presenting solutions; it also discusses the nitty-gritty of implementing them. Anyone looking for practical approaches to resolving the church's ills would do well to begin with this book."
**—Charles Zech, Center for Church Management and Business Ethics, Villanova University**

"Chris Lowney has combined his incredible love of the Church with his demonstrated management competence to help the entire Church not bemoan our challenges but combine our gifts with God's grace and be about building the kingdom. With integrity he names the problems and the opportunities and responsibilities each of us has to rediscover and reveal the splendor of our Church. The urgency of this is well described but so is the joy this journey can be."
**—Carol Keehan, president and CEO, Catholic Health Association**

"In *Everyone Leads*, Chris Lowney provides an excellent diagnosis of the complex challenges facing the Catholic Church in the United States and globally. More importantly, he shares a holistic strategy that every baptized Catholic can act on today to help the Church flourish, grow, and lead more people to Jesus. This book is a wonderful response to Pope Francis's invitation to all Catholics to be 'bold and creative in this task of rethinking the goals, structures, style and methods' of outreach by the Church."
—**Timothy C. Flanagan, founder and chair, Catholic Leadership Institute**

"With great respect for both Catholic beliefs and the hierarchy, Chris Lowney—a management expert and deeply committed Catholic—challenges clergy and laity to enliven the Church by living with the dedication Jesus expects of His disciples. This book is especially fresh because Lowney uses the language of leadership theory, not theology, to help his readers reinvigorate the institutional Church."
—**Michael Sheeran, SJ, president, Association of Jesuit Colleges and Universities**

"*Everyone Leads* is a profoundly inspiring gift to every person who recognizes the potential of the Catholic Church and the urgency to bring that potential to fruition. Chris Lowney elegantly blends analysis and spiritual reflection and delivers a blueprint for achieving a culture of accountability and entrepreneurial acumen in the Church. An invitation to co-responsibility for the Church's life and being, this is a prophetic contribution of great consequence."
—**Kerry Alys Robinson, founding executive director and global ambassador, Leadership Roundtable**

# EVERYONE LEADS
## How to Revitalize the Catholic Church

## CHRIS LOWNEY

ROWMAN & LITTLEFIELD
Lanham • Boulder • New York • London

Published by Rowman & Littlefield
A wholly owned subsidiary of The Rowman & Littlefield Publishing Group, Inc.
4501 Forbes Boulevard, Suite 200, Lanham, Maryland 20706
www.rowman.com

Unit A, Whitacre Mews, 26-34 Stannary Street, London SE11 4AB, United Kingdom

Distributed by NATIONAL BOOK NETWORK

British Library Cataloguing in Publication Information Available

Library of Congress Cataloging-in-Publication Data Available

ISBN 978-1-4422-6208-9 (cloth : alk. paper)
ISBN 978-1-4422-6209-6 (electronic)

♾™ The paper used in this publication meets the minimum requirements of American National Standard for Information Sciences—Permanence of Paper for Printed Library Materials, ANSI/ NISO Z39.48-1992.

*For the women and men who taught and guided me in grammar school, high school, university, and seminary. Thanks for what you gave so generously.*

# CONTENTS

# CHAPTER ONE

# Our Mighty Purpose

## *Creating the Twenty-First-Century Church*

"[T]HE TRUE JOY IN LIFE," WROTE PLAYWRIGHT GEORGE BERNARD SHAW, is working toward "a purpose recognized by yourself as a mighty one."

If Shaw is right, then these will be joyful decades for Catholics. For a mighty purpose awaits us. Our church is facing its greatest crisis in five centuries, and this book invites us to lead it forward. We are all co-responsible for the church's being and action, and it has never been more necessary for all of us to step in and lead.

Our church has such vast potential, so much of it lies untapped, and what we offer can mean so much to the world. We're not bringing sand to the Sahara, so to speak, but life-giving water to a society that is parched. We offer pathways to inner peace amidst a world that has grown noisy and media saturated. We stand beside the world's impoverished and marginalized amidst a culture that is increasingly bewitched by wealth. Contemporary culture champions the Darwinian struggle to get ahead; we instead preach service of others and the common good. Our divisive era pits one religion, ideology, political party, or tribe against another; we profess that our neighbors are all those in need, whatever their color or beliefs. Our first priority is not those with power and influence, but those who lack worldly status: the poor, jobless, refugees, persecuted, or infirm elderly.

Above all, we follow a path to salvation. Jesus is that path; our values are those he embodied. For sure, we have been very imperfect followers, but we can improve. And by doing so, by turning our church into what it can be, we will turn the world into what it should be. By rebuilding our church, we will renew the world.

But rebuild we must. We are the generation of Christians privileged to live at this inflection point in the church's history, the ones called to the mighty purpose of revitalizing the church and realizing its vast promise.

## The Church's Worst Crisis in Five Centuries?

The purpose is mighty, and so will be the effort required. Not only are we enduring a searing crisis, but our fortunes will deteriorate even further if current trends continue. Equally alarming is that many Catholics would scratch their heads and wonder: *Worst crisis in five centuries? What is this guy talking about?* That's frightening, because we cannot solve a problem that we do not even recognize. And we will not galvanize around new strategies unless we acknowledge that current ones are not working.

That's why this book will begin not with uplifting good news but with a bracing appraisal of our challenges, a call to action: the time has grown urgent for Catholics to show leadership and revitalize the church they love. The first thing that must change is our culture, the ways we think, operate, and make decisions. Such change never comes easily, above all to a church with a sacred tradition and a venerable history. For that reason, we must create a "burning platform" for change, a widespread conviction that the *status quo* is no longer sustainable. That burning platform for change is not yet ablaze in our church.

It ought to be. Even a cursory review of the landscape reveals the magnitude of our predicament. In one after another of the world's economically developed countries, church attendance has plummeted to historic lows, and tens of millions of adults have deserted Catholicism entirely. Not since the Protestant Reform, five centuries ago, has Catholicism suffered defections on so devastating a scale. And the future looks even grimmer: young adults show little interest in Catholicism (and in organized religion generally). Thousands of Catholic schools and parishes have been shuttered in the past few decades. The population of priests has been falling in multiple countries and is projected to shrink by almost another third in coming decades in the United States. And, at this worst possible moment, the Catholic hierarchy's credibility remains wounded by damaging pedophilia scandals.

The counter-narrative to this sorry portrait typically emphasizes the church's growth in the global South. Catholicism is the dominant religion across Latin America, for example, African Catholicism is enjoying extraordinary growth, and India has blessed the church with abundant religious vocations. All true, and that should thrill us: Africa's Catholic population has soared incredibly, almost tripling in the last few decades alone. Two-thirds of Catholics now live in the Southern Hemisphere. Catholicism has truly become a global church, which is a cause for great joy.

But the church of the Southern Hemisphere faces its own challenges. North Americans may lament their priest shortage, but the priest-per-Catholic ratios are drastically worse in virtually every African and Latin American country. And the percentage of those calling themselves Catholic in Latin America has been dropping for decades.

In sum, we are in trouble, all over the world, and the situation is urgent.

Equally worrisome is the lack of response to these challenges. Imagine a faulty but nonetheless revealing analogy: any major corporation that was losing customers at a similar pace would long ago have been catalyzed into an urgent quest for solutions. Everyone from chief executive to junior staff would know key facts and be enlisted in the fight to reverse the damaging trends. New approaches would be tested and their results monitored closely. Inexplicably, nothing like this is happening in our church.

Some readers will bristle at comparing the church to a "company" with "customers." They are right to be offended. We're not peddling laundry detergent to make money but offering something life-giving and deeply relevant to the world's sufferings. But that only reinforces the point: precisely because our mission is so profound, we ought to seek solutions and new approaches far more energetically and imaginatively than any worldly company would.

## THE TIME IS NOW URGENT FOR NEW APPROACHES

To be sure, there has been talk of urgency at the church's highest levels. More than four decades ago, Pope Paul VI wondered whether Catholicism was appropriately equipped to communicate its message well to the modern world and proclaimed the "urgency of giving a loyal, humble, and courageous answer to this question." But his urgent question remained unanswered nearly two decades later, when Pope John Paul II "sensed an urgent duty" to point out the "urgency" of revitalizing the church's outreach (yes, he referred to urgency twice in one paragraph). Elsewhere, he called for the church to find ways of speaking about our beliefs that would be "new in its ardor, methods, and expression." These urgent calls were not the hysterical bleats of attention-hungry television pundits but the sober perceptions of popes.

Yet few Catholics in the pews have been apprised that our situation is "urgent." Yes, initiatives like the New Evangelization were announced with great fanfare, but with no determined follow-through, no milestones or monitoring of outcomes, and, consequently, minimal impact: only a tiny percentage of the globe's Catholics could explain the initiative, much less their role in it. How could such torpor and complacency have taken root, while tens of millions have drifted from the Catholic Church?

Pope Francis seemed to understand that the time for new thinking is long overdue. His first major pronouncement, *Evangelii Gaudium*, frankly urged change. He said that the Church's pastoral efforts ought to "abandon the complacent attitude that says: 'We have always done it this way.'" The Pope invited all Catholics to be "bold and creative in this task of rethinking the goals, structures, style and methods" of outreach. He exhorted each bishop "to listen to everyone and not simply to those who would tell him what he would like to hear." He advised these shepherds to walk behind the flock from time to time, letting lay Catholics take the lead, "allowing the flock to strike out on new paths."

This book accepts the Pope's invitation to reject the "complacent attitude" of "we have always done it this way." Following chapters advocate a new culture of leadership for our church, a culture that will empower Catholics, unleash their talent, foster creativity and prudent risk-taking, and settle for nothing less than the highest professional standards in managing our church, because, as one leading Cardinal put it, "a church for the poor should not be poorly managed." Such a thoroughgoing transformation cannot succeed through the input of a few but will require the talents and commitment of all. In short, we must foster a culture where everyone leads.

Those ideas may feel radically, even dangerously, new. Radically different from the ways we've been doing things? For sure. But radically new? Hardly. The priorities proposed over coming chapters are the priorities articulated by Jesus, and the approach to mission is that of the earliest Christians. To thrive in this complex world, we don't have to drink some new twenty-first-century cocktail, we just need to drink more deeply from our own first-century well.

Granted, this book will employ some modern words and ideas that neither Jesus nor his early followers would have recognized, like leadership, strategy, accountability, or entrepreneurship. The apostles were blessed by the Holy Spirit at Pentecost, not with Harvard Business School educations. Still, whether by intuition or the Holy Spirit's guidance, our earliest leaders embodied all the traits that today's great leaders manifest: they were creative, took risks, adapted to new circumstances, unleashed each person's talents, never wavered from their core values, emphasized the mission above all, and acted courageously, thanks to the transformation that God's Spirit worked within them.

Still, some may read phrases like "new culture of leadership" and wonder whether this book intends to foment revolution or dissent in a church with clear teachings about hierarchy and teaching authority. No. No changes in church teaching are advocated in the following chapters, for two reasons. For one, that's not my role: I have opinions, like all thinking Catholics, but I'm not a canon lawyer or bishop, and I respect the church's teaching authority as a board member of one of her largest ministries.

But there's a second reason I won't wade into the quagmire of debating specific doctrines and practices. The church is unproductively mired in such squabbles, lurching inharmoniously from one discrete issue to another. Don't get me wrong: many of the pastoral or doctrinal topics debated are vitally important in their own right. But we never manage to rise from these piecemeal discussions; we don't refocus as a united church on the big picture. We never get around to confronting our overall predicament frankly and crafting a unifying, holistic approach to tackle it.

Instead, we've settled into Catholic tribes, each with its own favored websites, practices, and bishops, and each faction convinced that "those other" Catholics are responsible for the church's ills. Granted, such divisiveness almost invariably afflicts organizations with the onset of challenges. But healthy organizations get over the blame game once they appreciate that their house is crumbling around them; good leaders manage to rally the organization around its core mission and some unifying priorities in order to preserve what they all love. Yet decades have drifted by and that hasn't happened for us, suggesting an unfortunate failure of leadership, at multiple levels. Despite decades of discouraging trends, we've yet to forge revitalization strategies that everyone can understand and to which all can contribute.

## AN **EASTeR** STRATEGY TO REVITALIZE THE CHURCH

That's what this book will attempt. First will come the frank appraisal of our predicament, the "burning platform" for change. Then, we will rediscover the way of Jesus and learn lessons from Jesus's earliest followers. That will be the touchstone for all that follows: any worthy strategy for our future must be anchored in Jesus and our tradition. Upon that foundation, we will construct a strategy for revitalizing our church around five key principles; those fond of acronyms can fittingly call it our "EASTeR project." That is, our church will:

- Be more **Entrepreneurial**, more creative and innovative in everything we do.
- Be more **Accountable**. We will be good stewards who make best use of the talents and resources God has entrusted to the church; we will monitor our results, successes, and failures.

And we will emphasize three overarching priorities for action:

- **Serve** the world's poor and marginalized peoples.
- **Transform** the hearts and souls of our members.
- **Reach out** to engage and welcome the wider world.

Serve, transform, and reach out; do so with accountability and entre-preneurial flair. Those five ideas will unite Catholics, focus our efforts, revolutionize our approach to problems and opportunities, and give birth to a church that can thrive in the twenty-first century.

How do I guarantee that my master plan will work everywhere, from Manhattan to Manila? First, it's not *my* plan; it's Jesus's plan: the EASTeR project is solidly rooted in the gospels and inspired by the New Testament's vision for our church. And second, it's not a master plan. Rather, it's an invitation to become a more strategic church, imperative in this complex era. As for detailed master plans, the resourceful Catholics of Manila or Manhattan (or Madrid or Maputo) will surely know best how to enact our priorities in their own circumstances: our approach will empower rather than patronize local Catholic communities. As the mantra puts it: think globally, act locally.

And how do I guarantee that the EASTeR project will work? I don't. When organizations face complex, multifaceted challenges, no strategy is perfect. Rather, good strategies challenge great leaders to experiment with promising ideas, quickly replicating successes and har-vesting lessons learned from failures, all the while encouraging initiative to advance the mission. Our risk-averse church culture doesn't operate this way but now must. I hope this book will help spark a vibrant, ever-respectful, hopeful give-and-take, leading to a more joyful spirit of experimentation; to that end, each succeeding chapter will be followed by proposed discussion and action points, both for individual Catholics and for those in hierarchical authority.

Which raises another question. Who am I to propose how the church might better cope with the changing world? I don't claim to know the answers, but I've learned a bit about navigating institutional change by living through lots of it. I served as a managing director on three continents in an investment banking industry that was permanently convulsed by upheaval. We responded energetically, preserving the best of our venerable tradition while adapting thoroughly to the new environ-ment. Our church must do something analogous—the stakes so much higher because our mission is so much more important.

Now I am intimately involved in another transformation effort. The health care industry is racked by change, and I'm privileged to chair the board of one of Catholicism's (and America's) largest health care systems. Our hundred or so hospitals offer some $750 million in annual charity care to those in need, making us one of the church's largest charity providers. Our team feels deeply accountable for propelling the healing ministry of Jesus into the twenty-first century, and we are engineering the change needed to renew our timeless ministry.

Which gets to another vital credential for writing this book: I love the church for the good it does in the world and has done in my life. No institution, save my family, has given me more. I want the church to flourish not because it's my "home team" but because I believe in its truths and have experienced its life-transforming love. I was blessed in Catholic schools with a richer education than my parents could ever have afforded. I have nursed dying cancer patients to a dignified passing in a Catholic hospice, and, poignantly, helped accompany my own mother to her death at the same hospital. I have been consoled by faith in moments of grief, counseled by church men and women when uncertain, graced by our sacraments, and comforted by the familiar rhythms of Catholic worship when far away from home.

I have walked through one of the world's largest slums to visit impoverished tuberculosis sufferers who received life-saving medicines through a church-organized program, while AIDS orphans were receiving a life-changing education at a church school not far away. Pope Francis metaphorically envisioned a Catholic Church that tends the world's woes as a "field hospital" after battle, and I could not be more enthused about the riches our field hospital can bring to the world right now.

But to do that well, we need to renew ourselves. The Holy Spirit has placed us all here at this moment when our church stands at an inflection point: we can either stagnate or surge forward. None of us has asked for this calling; it has come to us, as calling so often does.

And that call has come not just to the Pope or bishops, which gets to a last introductory point, punctuating all else that has preceded it. This strategy, and its accompanying call to leadership, is for everyone and can be launched by anyone, by any single reader, parish, school, hospital, or diocese. Were it a top-down strategy that only the Pope and Vatican could put in motion, I would have respectfully written a private letter to the Holy Father. Rather, the book is intended to catalyze widespread discussion and action at all levels of the Catholic Church: we will not meet our manifold challenges unless we can deploy far more talent against them.

In secular terms, the book invites each of us to step up and seize his or her leadership opportunity and responsibility; in faith terms, each of us is called to answer the baptismal calling more dynamically. Our church's fortunes will improve when a pervasive culture of leadership takes root from top to bottom, but that leadership culture can fortunately be catalyzed from bottom to top, one individual, family, and Catholic institution at a time. The following chapter elaborates the urgency of creating this new leadership culture.

CHAPTER TWO

# Our Worst Crisis in Five Centuries?

ONLY A FOOL WOULD CLAIM INSIGHT INTO THE GLOBAL CHURCH'S challenges after visiting one parish. After all, every Catholic parish, school, hospital, and social service center tells its own consoling story of nourishing faith, serving the vulnerable, or accompanying the anguished.

Well, call me a fool. Because even though I visited countless Catholic institutions in nearly a dozen countries while writing this book, one parish visit all but encapsulated our church's crisis and promise.

That visit was to Blessed Sacrament parish, which anchors one end of a residential block in Queens, New York; the apartment building where I grew up anchors that block's other end. For a few years, that little block was more or less my world, at least until my parents first allowed me to cross a street on my own.

A verse from Yeats leapt to mind during the five minutes it took to walk that block nearly fifty years after my early childhood: "All has changed, changed utterly." Well, yes and no. Superficially, all the buildings look the same as when I entered Sr. Joan Maureen's first grade class in 1964. And the elegant Art Deco church still stands nearby. It seats 600, which probably seemed quite capacious when constructed in 1949 but quickly became too small: an "overflow" Sunday Mass in the school auditorium accommodated those who couldn't squeeze into the church's six or so Sunday Masses.

But the overflow Mass wasn't needed for long. We altar boys, perched up on the altar, could see pockets of empty seats growing larger with each passing year; one and then another Mass was dropped from the schedule;

and, over time, there were fewer parish priests. With fewer priests to track, we quickly learned each one's idiosyncrasies, who raced through weekday Masses in fifteen minutes, for example, and who playfully flicked wet fingers at us after water was poured over the priest's hands before the consecration.

The 7:00 a.m. weekday Mass had always been sparsely attended, save for our teachers, the Grey Nuns of the Sacred Heart, who floated (it seemed) through the church side door to fill the first two pews. But before long, there were fewer of them also; and we were startled at the start of one school year to see Sr. Rita Francis's flaming red hair as traditional habits gave way to modified ones.

But we weren't startled for long. She was still Sr. Rita Francis, even when she wore "regular clothes." Anyway, other changes seemed more important, like what new students had enrolled who might join touch football games that had long featured an Irish lineup of Mahers and Shanahans, until the advent of ethnic exoticism with Eddie Valdez in about third grade. Perhaps 10 percent of my classmates were Hispanic by the time we graduated in 1972; by my younger brother's graduation year, Hispanics may have comprised nearly half the class.

Still, some things seemed as if they would remain forever. Sr. Mary Patrick, the school principal since my second grade year, learned a smattering of Spanish and labored on for some thirty-five years, so much a neighborhood fixture that the street bordering the school building was rechristened "Sr. Mary Patrick Way."

Unfortunately, that street sign is all that remains of Blessed Sacrament School. Enrollment, more than 800 in my day, had fallen to around 200 by the time it closed in the early 2000s. Not that Jackson Heights was devoid of Catholic kids by then; rather, their Mexican and Central American day laborer parents could no longer afford a tuition that had risen beyond their modest reach. The school's economic viability had slowly evaporated, a story that has been repeated a few thousand times across Catholic America: more than 10,000 Catholic grammar schools thrived in 1965; barely 5,000 remain, and the number keeps shrinking.

My family had moved in the early 1980s, a year or so after my father had passed away. Father Steven had walked up the block from the rectory to administer the Anointing of the Sick, and an hour or so later, my father died in his own bed. What a blessed way to go.

One of the liturgical prayers from the funeral Mass seems relevant for our global church right now: "Life has changed, not ended." Life has not ended: Blessed Sacrament, and our church globally, is still a home for many, where the poor or vulnerable find compassion, and Catholics are nourished by the sacraments. But life has surely changed, in our church and in the world. And, much though I loved my Catholic boyhood, now frozen in idyllic memory like a village in a snow globe, I know that God is calling us to minister in different ways to a different world.

## CHALLENGES HAVE SNOWBALLED INTO CRISES

Unfortunately, we haven't figured out how to thrive in this new world. Too many seem to idealize our past rather than striving to flourish in this present moment that God has given us. It's time to heed the words of Ecclesiastes, "Do not say: How is it that former times were better than these? For it is not out of wisdom that you ask about this" (Eccles. 7:9). Amen to that. Let's give the present our wholehearted attention, for Blessed Sacrament parish turns out to have been a microcosm of our church at large, faced in country after country with challenges that have festered and are snowballing into a multidimensional crisis of historic proportions:

- Priest shortages, already debilitating almost everywhere in the world, will become even worse.

- As a result, our sacraments are becoming less available to the faithful, and scarcity is already turning to drought, a "sacramental emergency," in some pockets of the world. In many places, we cannot even offer the basic pastoral care mandated by Canon Law.

- Catholics are becoming less and less engaged with the church, in dozens of countries. An ever-shrinking percentage of the baptized even call themselves Catholic. Young adults, vital to our future, show little interest in organized religion.

- And all these unhappy trends are on track to worsen. In the developed countries of Europe, the Americas, or Oceania, for example, we've shown little ability to retain Catholic young adults or attract new adult members. And, in Africa and in other developing regions where the church is booming, we have not demonstrated that we can master the threats that arise as economies become fully developed.

Bottom line: we are witnessing trends that are utterly unsustainable. We cannot afford a few more decades like the ones we've just endured. Pope Benedict XVI once observed that our, "mission has taken on new forms and employed new strategies according to different places, situations, and historical periods," and this historical moment screams for new strategies. None of the church historians I consulted could remember such deterioration in the church's fortunes in so many countries simultaneously. The French Revolution, one opined, had ushered in a profound trauma for the church in various countries. But something so widespread? Maybe not since the sixteenth-century birth of Protestantism.

The rest of this chapter explores our sorry predicament. The rest of the book then explores the good news of a rejuvenation strategy.

## Too Few Priests for God's People

As my dying father's breathing grew shallow and raspy, Fr. Stevie had arrived to administer the Last Rites within minutes, but it's now taking longer and longer for a priest to arrive in most parts of the world. Soon after my stroll down memory lane at Blessed Sacrament, for example, my wife and I happened to be hiking national park trails in Utah. I was moved to praise God for our extravagantly beautiful planet and found the perfect place to do so: the St. Anthony in the Desert church stood within a few miles of our campground. It stood; it didn't stand out: I missed the small sign marking the church's turnoff and had to backtrack to find the tiny chapel, arriving a few minutes after the scheduled start time of the Saturday evening vigil Mass.

My wife and I quietly slid in the back door. I saw something I had never seen before at Mass: a woman was leading the service. Catholics? Or a renegade sect? I scanned the tiny congregation, concluded that I was not about to be kidnapped by a cult, and slipped into a pew. I recognized the familiar cadences of Catholic prayers. Yes, this church seemed to be one of "ours."

But it wasn't Mass. The woman was leading a communion service, something she did rarely, I concluded, because she paused once or twice when uncertain about the sequence of prayers; when she hesitated, her fellow Catholics pitched in to coach her forward. The team led itself quite well.

I chatted with her afterward. It turned out that the parish priest had called to say he was not coming and asked a parishioner to step up and lead a service. See, this priest must drive some 130 miles to reach that chapel, a fraction of the 500 miles he often logs each week as the sole priest tending a litany of five worship sites: St. Elizabeth, St. Jude, San Juan Diego, St. Anthony of the Desert, and, God bless Catholicism for this one: the Central Utah Correctional Facility.

Granted, sparsely populated and Mormon-heavy Utah is home to relatively few Catholics, but not long after, a speaking engagement took me to Wisconsin, which boasts one of America's highest proportions of Catholics outside the Northeast. I met the pastoral leader of St. Thomas the Apostle, a relatively new parish founded to replace and consolidate four rural parishes that had all been deemed nonviable and shuttered.

Like that Utah priest, St. Thomas's leader also shoulders a grueling schedule, with only one day off each week. But those long weeks, the parish's leader told me, are filled with the joy and the deep fulfilment that comes from being, "available to parishioners in their times of joys and sorrows. It enlivens my own faith life and calls me to be more of Jesus to them. The elderly and sick are especially close to my heart, and I try to visit them regularly, or see them when they are in hospitals or sickly at home."

Wow. What an ennobling vision. What energizing dedication. What team spirit, to be so dedicated to a purpose greater than one's own ego and advancement. I listened and thought: our church is going to thrive in this new century if we can find and promote many more leaders like this person.

Not that this person's role is without complications. See, St. Thomas's pastoral leader is not a "he." It's Sr. Marlita Henseler. She's not technically the pastor but a "pastoral leader," in the diocese's nomenclature. More than thirty parishes in that diocese have no resident priest; their pastoral leaders are permanent deacons, laypeople, and religious women like Sr. Marlita.

Many American Catholics already talk about "the priest shortage," but, as the cliché goes, you ain't seen nothin' yet. A tidal wave of priestly retirements is coming, and new ordinations are only about a third of what would be needed to replace those who retire or die. The experts at the Center for Applied Research in the Apostolate (CARA) estimate that within a couple of decades, we'll have about 25 percent fewer active diocesan priests than we do today. If it feels bad today, imagine a future of more parish closures and overworked priests straining to juggle multiple parishes.

Or maybe more foreign-born missionaries will come to plug the gap? These holy men have helped keep churches open, even if some have struggled mightily with cross-cultural challenges or with language gaps that diminish their effectiveness as preachers. Their presence can lull us into a terrible misperception: if those countries can afford to send priests "over here" to America, I guess they must have a priest surplus "over there," right?

Nothing could be more wrong, and in the new culture of leadership, we'll start thinking differently: there is no "over here" and "over there." We're one church, one body, as Paul put it. Accordingly, we'll think as much of the global church as we do of our own individual parish. Anyway, there is no priest surplus "over there." The relative priest scarcity is worse almost everywhere outside the United States. According to a recent edition of the Vatican's *Statistical Yearbook of the Church*, North America has one priest for every 1,762 Catholics. Africa? It's one for 4,948. South America? One for 7,008.

Those averages mask the worst cases. Consider Bishop Erwin Kräutler, who has one priest for every 25,000 Catholics in the Amazon rainforest region of Xingu. He deploys a mere twenty-seven priests across 800 worship sites. Do the math: that means one priest for every thirty worship sites across Xingu's vast expanse. As a result, the bishop explained, "our communities can only celebrate the Eucharist twice or three times a year at the most."

And many dioceses across Africa suffer priest shortages far worse than the continent's overall average. One could argue that our current approach is the exact opposite of what it should be. Organizations typically invest heavily in their most promising markets, and Africa is undoubtedly our fastest growing region. Yet we are steadily siphoning priests from a continent that is already under-resourced. As the scholar of religion Philip Jenkins put it: "It almost seems as if the church has scientifically assigned its resources to create the minimum possible correlation between priests and the communities that need them most."

But one often hears that seminaries are full in Africa, so won't Africa soon have enough priests both to ameliorate its own shortages *and* to keep plugging America's and Europe's gaps? Absolutely not. Yes, African vocations are booming, but at the current annual growth rate in the number of priests, it will take more than three decades for Africa's priest-per-Catholic ratio even to catch up to America's current (anemic-looking) priest-per-Catholic ratio.

There is, of course, much more to this story: the number of deacons, catechists, and lay ministers has been growing, almost exponentially in some parts of the world. And key to our revitalization strategy will be much more imaginative, expansive thinking about using this human talent to its utmost potential. But imagination can only help with part of our challenge. To state the obvious, deacons and lay ministers cannot celebrate Mass, which leads us to another worsening problem.

## A COMING PASTORAL DROUGHT?

See, as my father lay dying, only a priest could have anointed him sacramentally. And only a priest can celebrate Mass and consecrate the Eucharist—what the catechism calls "the source and summit of the Christian life."

Source and summit of Christian life: that's powerful imagery. Food is the "source" of physical life; if withdrawn, we die. Well, our spiritual nourishment is becoming harder to find, and sacramental deprivation is slowly turning to drought: in some parts of the world, Catholics feel lucky if they can attend a Mass even monthly. Cardinal Pietro Parolin, one of the Vatican's most senior officials as Secretary of State, acknowledged that the term "sacramental emergency" is now being used to describe the situation in some parts of South America, Africa, and even, shockingly, in pockets of Europe.

The solution is not a helicopter fleet to shuttle priests around lots of parishes each Sunday for fly in/fly out liturgies, because we are not just a Sacramental church but a sacramental one: that is, we are a sign of God's grace not only through the Eucharist but also by the love and pastoral care that should characterize our communities.

Remember Sr. Marlita, the pastoral leader in Green Bay? When I asked about her frustrations, she mentioned that she and other pastoral leaders "are the ones who know and are intimately connected with the lives" of the sick and elderly. She is the one who sits beside them as their loved ones slowly slip away to death. But when they pass, she acknowledges, the "priest coming to preside at the Mass does not know the individuals or families." She's merely stating a fact, not disparaging a priest who is undoubtedly holy and compassionate. The funeral Mass and Eucharist undoubtedly consoles the mourning family, but the human touch is diminished.

The Catholic Church is not supposed to function like this. That's not my opinion; the church's Canon Law plainly says that the parish priest is to "strive to know the faithful entrusted to his care. He is therefore to visit their families, sharing in their cares and anxieties and, in a special way, their sorrows. . . . He is to be especially diligent in seeking out the poor, the suffering, the lonely, those who are exiled from their homelands, and those burdened with special difficulties."

I'm so proud to belong to a church that enshrines such pastoral care as law, not simply as an extra that is nice to do when time permits. But even today, many priests cannot do what this canon instructs, and this pastoral care deficit will worsen as the priest population shrinks further. If we do not quickly reimagine our culture and each of our roles within the local church, our parishes will feel less and less vibrant pastorally. Even today, too many of the baptized are not being sufficiently fed, and it's showing: they are walking away from us. Hence our third interrelated problem, the declining participation among Catholics in the church's life:

## CATHOLIC PRACTICE: "DECLINING ALMOST EVERYWHERE" IN THE WORLD

Preceding paragraphs told a straightforward story: a widespread and worsening priest shortage, portending a "sacramental emergency" in some places. So here's a thought that seems counterintuitive, even illogical: what if, upon closer examination, there is no priest shortage at all?

That provocative conclusion was posed by Paul Sullins, a Catholic priest and sociologist at the Catholic University of America, who crunched the nationwide numbers on sacramental participation. Yes, Sullins noted, if all you do is compute the ratio of priests to America's baptized Catholics, you see a steadily worsening shortage: fewer and fewer priests to cover more and more baptized Catholics.

But what if you analyzed it as an economist would measure supply and demand? Instead of calculating priests per Catholics, what if one calculates "priests per Mass-goers"? Take the Brooklyn Archdiocese, which numbers some 1.5 million Catholics. Only a small minority of them attend Mass each Sunday. According to the Archbishop, "our Mass-going population in Brooklyn and Queens is between 17 and 13%. Older Catholics can remember when the number was above 60%." And New York's Cardinal Dolan has fretted over the same phenomenon: "I am a realist, and we're in big trouble. An old proverb in the Church claims, 'No Eucharist, no Church.' The scholars tell us that most of our Catholic people no longer go to Sunday Mass."

Bottom line? The "demand" for the Eucharist, the quintessential "service" delivered by priests, has been falling even more precipitously than the supply of priests, in many places. And the demand for the sacrament of Reconciliation has plummeted at a far more accelerated pace. Baptisms, first communions, marriages: all down. If you look at it that way, there is no shortage at all.

Thus a horrific irony is slowly coming to pass: even though the number of priests has been declining, from one ghastly perspective, there is no priest shortage, because the "demand" for the sacraments has been falling even more sharply. Needless to say, none of us takes comfort in that fact. It says something dreadful about the health of our church that so few Catholics even bother to partake in the "source and summit" of our life. As the sociologist Fr. Sullins ruefully concluded: "the absence of a clergy crisis is a much more serious problem than the presence of one."

Of course it is. If a handful of Catholics don't show up for Mass, we might uncharitably wonder why they're lazy or not getting it. But when 70 percent and more of all baptized Catholics are not showing up, it's time to start wondering what *we're* not getting, what message the Holy Spirit is trying to convey to us. Why is it that fewer and fewer Catholics feel engaged by the church? The greatest threat to Catholicism's future, then, may not be the dwindling supply of priests but the dwindling number of Catholics who deem the church relevant to their lives.

Granted, the preceding discussion has focused disproportionately on the United States, and a few readers may think: *what a shortsighted American, and how disloyal to the church, to highlight some bad news in the United States and then claim that the whole Catholic globe is troubled.* Sorry, what's shortsighted and disloyal is that reaction, which invites complacency and denial. A detailed treatment of every country is impossible in a book of this sort, but it doesn't take reams of data to confirm that our challenges are indeed global. Start with what the Vatican's own statisticians have observed, encapsulated in the opening sentence of a Catholic News Service story: "The percentage of Catholics practicing their faith is declining almost everywhere around the globe."

That blunt assessment was summarizing research from the Vatican's Central Office for Church Statistics, which had noted: "a weakening of faith in Christian communities ... an individualistic approach to belonging to the church, a decline in religious practice and a disengagement in transmitting the faith to new generations."

Take Latin America, vital to our future as home to nearly 40 percent of the world's Catholics. But the percentage of Latin Americans who call themselves Catholic has been inexorably slipping for decades, from above 90 percent to below 79 percent. In Brazil, the world's largest Catholic country, the percentage of Catholics has now dropped all the way to 60 percent, prompting Cardinal Cláudio Hummes's anguish: "We wonder with anxiety: how long will Brazil remain a Catholic country?"

It's far worse in Europe, where the late Cardinal Franz König of Vienna opened a 1999 address with this succinct assessment: "Europe, previously the heartland of the Western Church, is now being described as 'the most godless quarter on earth.'" France, Spain, and Germany, for example, together account for nearly a hundred million Catholics, yet the church's future is imperiled in all three countries: less than 15 percent of Catholics attend Mass; priestly and religious life vocations have plummeted; and churches are closing.

## THINGS WILL GET WORSE, NOT BETTER

We are verging on crisis. Never has there been such a sustained decline in so many countries in sacramental participation or Catholic identity. What's more, the institutions where individuals meet us and learn about us are also dwindling: the number of schools has plummeted in the United States, and many parishes are struggling for viability—more concerned about maintenance and survival than outreach.

And nothing indicates an imminent rebound. Pope Benedict XVI reminded us that the modern church must grow "by attraction," yet here in the United States, we've demonstrated no meaningful ability to attract. Pew Research found that we manage to attract only one adult convert for every six adult Catholics who walk away from the church. Meditate on that statistic for a moment—six leave for every one that joins. Imagine a business that was losing six customers for each new one it landed; it would not remain in business for long. And our "Six out/one in" ratio is far worse than virtually every other Christian denomination in that same study; indeed, evangelical churches are thriving as net winners, attracting more members than they lose.[22]

We're not attracting new members, and we're not even retaining our own beloved children in our fold. Look around most Catholic congregations on Sunday morning. Chances are, you will see lots of greying hair, like mine. What you won't see are many young adults. Consider this sobering finding by Christian Smith, the distinguished sociologist of religion at Notre Dame: "fully one-half of [US] youth who self-identified as Catholic as teenagers no longer identified as Catholics 10 years later in their 20s. That is a 50 percent loss through attrition in one decade." And it's not like the remaining 50 percent turn out to be strong Catholics. The same researcher found that only 7 percent of one young adult cohort he studied could be called "practicing" Catholics in any traditional sense. The research is crystal clear: those who leave the church are most likely to do so in late teen and early adult years. Yet, maddeningly, as you review church programs, you are unlikely to find many outreach programs to engage and enfranchise these vulnerable young people. We're letting our future slip away without even putting up much of a fight.

So, why isn't the American church shrinking rapidly? There's a one-word explanation: Hispanics. The United States counts forty million more Hispanics today than just a few decades ago, and, if not for Hispanic immigration, as respected journalist John Allen put it bluntly, "the Catholic church in America would be contracting dramatically."

But no one can guarantee that the grandchildren of these Hispanic immigrants will remain loyal. Nearly a quarter of adult Latinos in the United States call themselves *former* Catholics; many of these left Catholicism because they were seeking a "more personal relationship with Jesus," and found it not with us but at Pentecostal or Evangelical churches (a phenomenon, by the way, that is happening all across Latin America and in many pockets of Africa). All of that augurs poorly for our future.

## Transformation Begins with a Sense of Crisis

A few readers may bridle that traditional markers of Catholic identity have so dominated this chapter's discussion. Lots of good Catholics, they may object, don't make it to church every Sunday: why is Mass attendance such an important barometer? And many of those who leave Catholicism find wonderful Christian homes in other denominations: why is that a terrible thing, as long as their relationship to Jesus deepens? And, anyway, Jesus' message is about serving the poor, not about tallying up more converts than other denominations.

Those points have validity, and service to poor communities will later emerge as a key strategic priority. But, simply put, we won't have Catholic ministries without Catholics. Half-empty, understaffed churches with aging or lukewarm members will neither sustain themselves nor our charitable efforts, much less conceive bold initiatives for a changing world. More fundamentally, if we really believe that we have something good, true, and beautiful to offer the world, we should want to see it flourish, yet we verge on a vicious cycle of stagnation leading to never-ending retrenchment.

That's a lot of gloomy news. I plead guilty to violating one of Napoleon's leadership principles: "A leader is a dealer in hope," the emperor purportedly once said. Could I have told a more hopeful story? You bet. I could fill books with hopeful stories, like the explosive growth in the number of deacons, catechists, and lay Catholics who now keep our church running. I could tell great stories about our many wonderful priests, and how satisfied most parishioners are with their local pastors. Without all these, the great majority of the church's activities would have long ago collapsed.

And my many Filipino, Korean, Indian, and African friends would wave their hands and wonder if I have forgotten about their vibrant churches. Across Africa, for example, the number of Catholics has surged by 238 percent, to 199 million. That's not the total growth over the last century; that, incredibly, is the growth since 1980 alone. Over the same time frame, the number of parishes has doubled. Those happy trends will continue into the foreseeable future.

And here's more good news: our church is the world's largest charity provider; we enjoy a two-thousand-year tradition, count adherents in nearly 200 countries, and are visibly unified through the Papal office. We can and will revitalize ourselves if we imaginatively leverage these and other vast resources.

But if I haven't followed Napoleon's dictum by accentuating these positives, it's because I believe in what might be called "Gerstner's Law." Lou Gerstner, the legendarily successful executive who some years ago resurrected the IBM company from almost certain ruin, once spoke of the essential first step toward revitalizing any challenged organization: "Transformation of an enterprise begins with a sense of crisis or urgency. No institution will go through fundamental change unless it believes it is in deep trouble and needs to do something different to survive."

He's right. We are not yet behaving as if we understand that we are "in deep trouble and need to do something different." Russell Shaw, who long served as director of media relations for what was then called the National Conference of Catholic Bishops, wrote, "Sad to say, many Church leaders also close their eyes, at least in public, to the abundant evidence of decline. Perhaps they fear that openly acknowledging the magnitude and seriousness of the crisis would hurt morale and only speed up the collapse." I can't say whether Shaw's assessment is accurate: he was an insider; I'm not. But I can say this: troubled organizations need to catalyze change by sharing the facts frankly and soliciting solutions widely. If, instead, they overemphasize the positive, they drift into defensiveness, denial, and complacency.

Or they latch on to overly simplistic solutions. One often hears the argument, for example, that our fortunes would improve dramatically if only we trumpeted the church's teachings unambiguously and confronted secular culture more forthrightly; that clarity, it's sometimes argued, would rally adherents and attract new members.

Except the evidence doesn't seem to bear out that theory. It takes nothing from St. John Paul II's remarkable achievements to observe that while he may have tamed communism, he couldn't tame modernity. He was the undisputed champion of forceful, unambiguous church teaching, yet he couldn't reverse the church's decline across Europe or even within his own beloved Polish homeland. Yes, Poles love John Paul II, but fewer and fewer Poles love going to Mass. More than 60 percent of them attended weekly Mass in the early 1990s; now the figure has slid to around 40 percent nationally and far less in urban Warsaw. Vocations to the priesthood and religious life have plummeted. A Polish religious broadcaster summed it up succinctly: "Twenty years of freedom and religion is evaporating. This is the crisis of Christianity in Poland." How could that have happened, when Poland scrupulously followed the "unambiguous orthodoxy playbook," led by priests and bishops who promulgated church teachings clearly?

What went wrong is straightforward, yet devilishly complex: modernity (or "postmodernity," or any other label of your preference).

The church helped deliver Poland's free society but was ill-equipped to compete in it. Individualism and consumerism took root; Poles were inundated with advertising and messaging that celebrate the freedom to buy what one desires, sleep with whom one wants, and make one's own moral choices. As making money to afford a better lifestyle became a prime objective, career-minded Poles moved to bigger cities; attachments to traditional values loosened.

The phenomenon is not unique to Poland. As economies develop and postmodern values take root, cultural trends often emerge that are inimical to organized religion. Scholars like Robert Barro, Rachel McCleary, Paulo Reis Mourão, and others have studied the negative correlation between economic development and religious practice. As countries become more prosperous, religious vocations almost always tend to decrease; so does attendance at religious services. That seems to have happened in the United States, Europe, and Australia, and now in Latin America, Poland, and elsewhere.

So what does the Catholic future look like in rapidly developing regions of Africa, India, and elsewhere? Let's hope the churches there figure out (and teach the rest of us) how the church can thrive in an individualistic, consumerist, secular, postmodern world. But we don't have the answers yet, and one can see challenges for the African church, for example, as Pentecostal churches attract more and more Catholics.

Yes, the Catholic Church has grown exponentially in Africa, but expert statisticians attribute most of that growth to the continent's high birthrate, not to our ability to attract and retain new adult members. Plainly put, the answer to the question, "why will the African church still be thriving in twenty years?" cannot simply be "because it is thriving now." In light of the church's history elsewhere, that complacent mindset would be either arrogant or naïve.

## IT'S TIME FOR "LOYAL, HUMBLE, AND COURAGEOUS" ANSWERS

Our fundamental challenge is just as Pope Paul VI articulated it way back in 1973: "The conditions of the society in which we live oblige all of us therefore to revise methods, to seek by every means to study how we can bring the Christian message to modern man. . . . does the Church or does she not find herself better equipped to proclaim the Gospel and to put it into people's hearts with conviction, freedom of spirit and effectiveness? We can all see the urgency of giving a loyal, humble and courageous answer to this question, and of acting accordingly."

The intervening decades have answered that question for us: no, we are not "better equipped" to "proclaim the Gospel and put it into people's hearts." The statistics speak for themselves. We haven't cracked the code of speaking to modern men and women.

Granted, the church thinks in centuries, as the old cliché puts it, and the worst reaction would be to jettison our defining traditions and truths based on some statistics. But the church can also suffer for centuries for missteps or inaction; the decades surrounding the Protestant Reform are a perfect example of problems neglected until full-blown disaster erupted for institutional Catholicism (although, thankfully, not for Christianity; we are enriched by the witness and traditions of our Protestant brothers and sisters).

Even a church that thinks in centuries must now acknowledge that we cannot afford another century of these trends; we already risk becoming, as Pope Francis put it, "mere onlookers as the Church gradually stagnates." It's already hard enough, for example, to keep wavering teenagers interested in the church, even when both parents are practicing Catholics; imagine, thirty years into the future, how difficult it will be to interest the teenaged children of a generation of parents who rarely attend church themselves. Inaction today could cost us for generations.

This book rejects the roads to stagnation, like pretending that the approaches of recent decades have been working, or will work if only we give them just a few more years. Let's not resign ourselves to slow decline, claiming that we're doing as well as we can in a secular age. And let's not hunker down to shake our fists at modernity, like medieval monks who retreat behind monastery walls while the barbarians ravage the landscape. Jesus loved, healed, and engaged the complex world into which he was born, and we are surely called to do the same.

Ultimately, Napoleon was right: leaders must be dealers in hope, and this book will now be pulled forward, chapter after chapter, by the conviction that a strategy for revitalizing ourselves is within reach, but only if we summon the mettle to strike out along new strategic paths.

The first step in that direction has been this chapter's subject: the willingness to face the facts squarely and share them widely, without yielding to the unhelpful instincts either to paint the best possible picture or to paint other Catholics as the villains. Organizations in denial don't thrive, nor do organizations succeed by playing the blame game. They succeed by collaborating to find solutions to their problems.

The second step in the right direction is the humility to admit that we don't have answers to many challenges that confront us. Now is not the moment for our shepherds to assure us paternalistically that the winning plan is in place. Now is the moment to explain the magnitude of our challenges, to enlist the broad community of the faithful to help conceive new approaches, and to experiment with promising ideas that might emerge from the grassroots.

That gets to the most important step, and the following chapter's subject. We need to flip this chapter's mindset upside down. That is, instead of focusing first on a shortage of priests, we're going to focus first on what is abundant—hundreds of millions of talented Catholics whose gifts have not been fully utilized. Instead of reactively cobbling together patchwork responses to our challenges, we'll proactively create strategies that unleash the energies and imaginations of these many Catholics. In short, we need to create a new culture of leadership, where those in authority call and empower lay Catholics to lead, and where each person hears and answers that call to lead.

## Pray, Reflect, Discuss, and Act

This book hopes to catalyze discussion and action, in all sectors of the church. Accordingly, each chapter is followed by questions and ideas. Most of these will invite "bottom up" leadership: that is, individuals, small groups, or leadership teams could pray over and act on the proposed point. A few of the suggestions, however, call for "top down" leadership, that is, bishops or other hierarchical authorities would have to take the initiative. The questions and ideas may sometimes feel most relevant to parishes, but essential to our new culture of leadership will be a "one church mindset" across all ministries, where Catholic schools, universities, hospitals, or social service agencies would also show "ownership" by discussing and addressing the church's challenges in the broadest sense. The questions for this chapter are:

- The chapter outlined profound challenges faced by the global church: how does the church look from where you sit? That is, in your parish (or diocese, or school), it seems worse? Better? Have you noticed other challenges that the chapter didn't even touch upon?

# CHAPTER THREE

# Everyone Leads

## *Imagining the Church's New Culture of Leadership*

I SET OUT TO WRITE A BOOK ABOUT REVITALIZING THE INSTITUTIONAL church, but the book that emerged is as much about embracing our individual calling.

For sure, this book explores how a big, global church must think and act differently to fulfill more effectively the mission that Jesus gave us. And while some of what follows is what a Pope, a bishop, or diocesan leaders could do differently, more of what follows concerns the other 1.2 billion of us.

Put plainly—every one of us must show more leadership. If we "get" that, as a church we will thrive; if we don't get that, we will continue to struggle. Strong leadership from bishops will ultimately mean little if the rest of us aren't leading well. Conversely, if a critical mass of us can lead as we are capable, our church will flourish, even if (God forbid), we get lousy leadership from those in hierarchical authority.

Granted, that assertion is so alien to our accustomed thinking that it may seem ludicrous. What can it mean that everyone must show leadership? That a billion of us ought to parade around wearing bishops' miters or dash off encyclicals about doctrines we don't like? No, and the very fact that we don't easily envision our church leadership roles indicates just how impoverished our concept of leadership has become. So we need to start by better understanding what leadership means; we'll draw on the dictionary (what could be more basic?), the experience of successful institutions, and, most importantly, our own Catechism, recent Popes, and Jesus.

When invited to lecture on leadership, I use a simple exercise to surface misguided assumptions. I ask attendees to name a few living leaders. The audience invariably focuses on the famous and powerful: their company's chief executive, the Pope, or America's president. Then I ask who had thought of their own name; everyone laughs: *Yeah, right, who is a leader? The Pope, the president, and me. Good one.*

But I'm serious. Take one common dictionary definition of leadership: to point out a way, direction, or goal; and to influence others toward it. Well, isn't it true that every one of us does those words, all the time? We parents are "pointing out a way" for children; we are role modeling virtues like patience, hard work, or fairness; we are influencing these children by what we say and do. The same is surely true for our lives as Catholics—we are pointing a way and influencing children or neighbors through the seriousness of our commitment, for example, to prayer, charity, justice, personal morality, and the other hallmarks of Christian discipleship. By the dictionary definition, we are leading, well or poorly, all the time. As the great humanitarian Albert Schweitzer once put it, "Example is not the main thing in influencing others; it is the only thing."

Everyone leads.

That's not rah-rah, motivational claptrap. Rather, the world's most sophisticated corporations understand a simple truth that we as a church must now grasp: widely distributed leadership, what this chapter calls our "new culture of leadership," has become essential to organizational success. An anecdote will illustrate why.

## THE WAY FORWARD: EVERYONE LEADS

I was once invited to address a few dozen leaders at a division of General Electric (GE), one of the world's most admired companies. I reviewed their leadership-related messaging to employees, and two simple ideas stood out. "The world is changing faster than ever," one of their presentations stated, and another slide drew the natural conclusion that every organization is therefore "being challenged to think, act, and lead in new ways." Specifically, "Everyone is a leader." Simply put—the world is changing fast; we must think in new ways; therefore, everyone leads.

I lived through the birth of that organizational logic. When someone used the word "leadership" way back when I started working in investment banking, what invariably came to our minds was a person, J. P. Morgan's chief executive. And our 1983 world was still stable enough that the CEO and his inner circle could make the crucial decisions and publicly represent the company wherever needed.

But as complexity and change engulfed us, we no longer had time to refer every important decision to the big bosses; and, anyway, those closer to the ground were often better suited to address the challenge at hand. Someone else besides the CEO frequently had to show leadership, and "someone else" soon became "everyone else." Our fundamental concept of leadership evolved; the word no longer connoted a person sitting atop the hierarchical heap but a mindset and behavior needed from everyone.

Our top executives didn't become less important or lose their authority. Our chief executive was still, pardon the analogy, as much our corporate "pope" as before, minus the infallible pronouncements, white zucchetto, and much else. His role was not diminished, but our roles were augmented. We weren't stealing slices from the boss's leadership pie, so to speak, but baking a new and bigger leadership pie. We knew that we needed to feast on more leadership behavior if we were to surmount the increasingly broad array of challenges that confronted us. That's just what our church will need to do.

Initially, we had trouble wrapping our heads around this new way of thinking. It entailed a massive culture change. We had long enjoyed the fruits of highly centralized leadership. Suddenly, we felt like left-handed people who had to become ambidextrous. We didn't want to chop off our left hand—we still wanted centralized leadership where appropriate. The CEO (or the Pope and bishops in the church's case) would still make the decisions appropriate to them.

But we wanted to wield our right hand more adeptly by empowering the rest of the team as much as possible. That didn't come naturally. Some bosses found it difficult to delegate—they wanted to control everything, make all the decisions, and have the last word in every discussion, even when others might have had far more relevant expertise and experience for the question at hand. Conversely, some bosses delegated well, but subordinates shrank from the leadership asked of them. They were too comfortably ensconced in the passive role of letting someone else make the tough decisions and take initiatives. Such subordinates had been molded in a paternalistic culture where the boss always decided, and they could not grow into the new culture we needed. Unfortunately, all the above holds equally true of our church—the very same obstacles are standing in the way of developing the new leadership culture we need.

To be sure, our church is neither GE nor J. P. Morgan. We should not do things just because big companies are doing them (in fact, a few readers will undoubtedly believe that if multinational conglomerates are heading one way, we ought to be running fast in exactly the opposite direction). But our Catholic tradition, if we scrutinize it carefully, will yield exactly the same conclusions about widely distributed leadership.

It doesn't seem that way at first glance. So much of our culture seems to reinforce the very opposite. For example, we speak of a Holy Father, the pope who alone dresses in white and is the sole source of infallible pronouncements on faith and morals; how's that for an unambiguous signal about centralized leadership? Or how about what St. Pius X said in his encyclical *Vehementer Nos*, "the Church is essentially an unequal society . . . the Pastors and the flock . . . the one duty of the multitude is to allow themselves to be led, and, like a docile flock, to follow the Pastors."

Thankfully, no Pope or bishops are out there championing that century-old quote, but it speaks to a history that has almost exclusively reinforced images of hierarchical authority. And, without doubt, in many respects, church leadership is hierarchical. Canon law reserves many authorities exclusively for priests, bishop, or Pope.

## WE EACH HAVE A PRIESTLY, PROPHETIC, ROYAL MISSION

That's why the church's theologians and hierarchical leaders must now work hard to strengthen our atrophied right hands, that is, our universal call to lead. We can start by pondering the Catechism's powerful assertion about the baptized: "By Baptism, they share in the priesthood of Christ, in his prophetic and royal mission."

That excerpt is not my license to stand up and preside at Mass—everyone understands that there are different roles in the church. But words like king, prophet, and priest are not empty rhetoric. They have profound meaning and imply a leadership responsibility. We have not yet fully explored the leadership implications of this baptismal call for all women and men in the church.

Recent popes have encouraged us to do so. Consider, for example, Pope Benedict XVI's statement: "it is necessary to improve pastoral structures in such a way that the co-responsibility of all the members of the People of God in their entirety is gradually promoted. . . . This demands a change in mindset, particularly concerning lay people. They must no longer be viewed as 'collaborators' of the clergy but truly recognized as 'co-responsible,' for the Church's being and action."

Pope Benedict, a cautious scholar, never tossed words around sloppily. By calling us to be "co-responsible," he was effectively calling us to show more leadership (and calling those with hierarchical authority to open up space and structures for this to happen). Many of us, for example, know what it means to be "responsible" for the "being and action" of one's child; it entails proactive involvement in decisions about the child's life and ongoing oversight of the child's upbringing. Well, co-responsibility for the church's being and action implies similarly proactive participation.

Benedict wasn't the first pope to use the "r-word"; Pope John Paul II had called American bishops to: "a commitment to creating better structures of participation, consultation and shared responsibility." And Pope Francis, in his own down-to-earth way, rendered all that papal-ese into vivid imagery in *Evangelii Gaudium*: "[the bishop] will sometimes go before his people, pointing the way and keeping their hope vibrant. . . . At yet other times, he will have to walk after them, helping those who lag behind and—above all—allowing the flock to strike out on new paths." The image of the bishop, "leading from behind," so to speak, will feel novel to most of us. So will its corollary: that the rest of us must exhibit the will and imagination to strike out on new paths, as appropriate. That should come "above all," Francis said.

This vision of bishops who both lead and follow may sound revolutionary but is a paradox as old as our faith tradition. We Christians, for example, call ourselves "followers" of Jesus, and our religious language uses words with connotations of follower-ship, like "disciple" and "vocation." The Latin root of "disciple," for example, connotes a pupil or follower. But our religious language also uses words with the opposite connotation, like "apostle" and "mission." The roots of those words connote "sending." And when I send you somewhere, you're not following; you're striking out and forging the way ahead.

That's the dynamic of Christian life: we lead and follow. If we do only one or the other, we are not fully living our call. That is, our leadership must be rooted in Jesus, followership of Jesus's way and of our church's beliefs. But, at the same time, if we do not see ourselves as apostles on mission, who are forging ahead as leaders, we are not embracing our full call. And if those in formal governance roles, like priests and bishops, are not expanding opportunities for lay talent to lead, then they are not fulfilling their roles either.

## Hey America, Let's Catch Up with Kenya

Jesus often reinforced his points through images and parables, so we might picture our new culture of leadership by looking at Lucy Kungu, Peter Karanja, and Samuel Waweru in action; they are the first of various leaders who will be profiled in this and following chapters.

I traveled a long way to interview these three, some 7,300 miles from New York to Nairobi. The last few miles were the most picturesque, in a car that glided under blooming Jacaranda trees, rattled over potholed dirt lanes, dodged one or two small goat herds, and bypassed the "Hot Motel," a roadside shack that seemed to specialize in frenzied hourly stays rather than restful overnight ones.

Eventually, one reaches St. Joseph the Worker church, or, better put, the guard who opens the big metal gate in the tall concrete wall that surrounds the church. Not that the church isn't welcoming: St. Joseph's ministers to vulnerable children, unschooled youth, the sick, poor families, and countless others. Ironically, the gated, walled St. Joseph's seems far more open and welcoming than many American churches with wide-open doors.

Though the church is welcoming, its neighborhood is insecure, hence the precautions. Some 650,000 people are crammed into Nairobi's Kangemi district, many living in one-room wooden shacks and surviving on jobs that can be here today and gone tomorrow, say as manual laborers on small construction sites or as house cleaners in Nairobi's more upscale neighborhoods. Since livelihoods are precarious, so too is the neighborhood.

But my visit there was not poverty tourism, a prelude to describing benighted souls in dire straits and plaintively pleading that we privileged folks condescend to help them. No. This story is about what they can do for us. Kangemi's Catholics seem far ahead when it comes to creating our church's new culture of leadership; they show us leadership in action and implicitly challenge the rest of us to catch up.

The previous chapter quoted Canon Law 529's instruction that pastors should "be especially diligent in seeking out the poor, the suffering, the lonely, those who are exiled from their homeland, and those burdened with special difficulties." Well, just about every one of Kangemi's 20,000 Catholics is either "poor, exiled, sick, or burdened with special difficulties," whether financial or otherwise. To honor that canon law would require far more parish priests than the archdiocese will ever have available.

Globally, countless parishes now find themselves in that situation, but St. Joseph's did something rather than benignly neglect its marginalized, as often happens when staff-short parishes lapse into a maintenance mode, which quickly degenerates into stagnation as spiritually unfulfilled parishioners start drifting away. To avoid that, St. Joseph's heeds another mandate in canon law, which instructs parish priests to "recognize and promote the specific role which the lay members of the faithful" have in the church's mission.

And that brings us to Peter, Lucy, and Samuel. Each of them leads one of the parish's many *jumuiyas*, shorthand for the Kiswahili phrase, *Jumuiya Ndogo Ndogo za Kikristoor*, that is, small Christian communities. The parish priests can't humanly manage all the pastoral care and community leadership that Kangemi needs, but Peter, Lucy, Samuel, and their fellow jumuiya leaders sure can. Samuel tells me that his jumuiya meets after the Sunday noon Mass, when about two dozen people gather: "we pray, we share the Word, we say the rosary." Each person in turn, "shares the challenges," that the Sunday gospel has presented to them. "If a member of the jumuiya is sick, we visit them, to encourage them. We take prayers, or some sugar or milk to the sick person." The description brings to mind those inspiring early Christian communities depicted in Acts of the Apostles.

The meetings rotate from one household to another each week, but I look at those one-room shacks and I wonder how that could work: "Forgive me for saying it, but the houses I see seem too small to fit so many people." Peter tries not to sound patronizing as he answers this American *mzungu* (slang for white person) who doesn't seem to get it, "Well, we each bring a chair from our homes, and we form a circle *outside* the house of the person where we are meeting." What a powerful witness it must be, I think, as they all sit together and share while their neighbors bustle by.

And if it rains? Kangemi's lanes are unpaved, after all, and Nairobi is a notoriously rainy city. They laugh in unison, "Don't worry, somehow we all squeeze inside together into the house. It seems impossible, but we do it."

These jumuiya leaders are not parish priests, but they get some of the same rewards, which is to say, the same frustrations. The jumuiya leader and members, for example, are the ones who first vet whether adult baptismal candidates are taking their Christian responsibilities seriously. So eager candidates will be unfailingly faithful jumuiya participants in the run-up to baptism. After that? They will still attend Mass, but some melt away from the jumuiya meetings. As Lucy puts it: "They don't need you; you never see them."

"It is not an easy job to be a leader," says Lucy, "because people have different opinions." She taught grammar school for years, and dealing with little kids probably prepared her well to cope with us grown-up babies. "I didn't want to be a leader," she tells me, but as she elaborates, I see how terrifically well suited she actually is for church leadership: "Sometimes you feel like God is calling you," she says. Once, while attending Eucharistic Adoration, the feeling of the call felt so palpable to her that, she concluded, "if this is the call of the Lord, I will go to the end."

The others nod as she tells this story. Each has known not only the frustrations of leadership but also its consolations. Peter talks of visiting neighborhood families and identifying candidates for the parish's "vulnerable children" program of feeding and tutoring: "For me, it is really touching. And seeing what happens to the children who enter the program, it really gives me hope." Indeed, these visits to the poorest members of their already-poor community seem to transform their own hearts: "Sometimes," Peter says, "you become so moved that you chip in your own money," to support a poor child who can't be accommodated by the vulnerable children program.

As I drive away from Kangemi, it's not just Nairobi's blooming Jacaranda trees that are vivid. So is the new culture of leadership. What powerful role models these jumuiya leaders are for the rest of us. I think of the naturalness with which Lucy, Peter, and Samuel referred to themselves as leaders, perceived themselves as leaders, and acted as leaders. I compare the expansive ways in which their gifts are used against our own relatively narrow concept of leadership in so many parishes. Say "leader," and we think of Pope or bishop, not ourselves. Say "contribute," and we think of our money more than our talents. Say "pastoral care," and we think of the priest, not of ourselves. We may see ourselves as lectors, ushers, or parish council members; our brothers and sisters in Kangemi challenge us to imagine myriad more ways in which we could serve and lead. And we'll have to start imagining new ways to deploy more of our talent if we hope to meet the mounting challenges we face.

They've got something that we badly need. I'm not talking about transplanting Kangemi's jumuiya system to the United States. American Catholics grow impatient if it takes five minutes to maneuver out of a crowded parish parking lot after Mass; I don't see us adding a three-hour jumuiya sharing to Sunday observance. But I'm talking about the spirit of their jumuiyas, the co-responsibility for the church that is exemplified in deeds, not just talked about in words. Catholics like Lucy, Peter, and Samuel are sitting in every congregation in the world. Too often, their leadership potential remains untapped. Just as Africa conceived the jumuiya to build the church within its culture, we too must find imaginative ways to unleash each Catholic's gifts.

There is, of course, a complementary piece of the new leadership puzzle. Fr. Tom Sweetser is head of the Parish Evaluation Project, and I asked him what characterizes thriving parishes: "Pastor, pastor, pastor," he said, "That still is the most important ingredient." Sweetser wasn't referring to pastors who believe they must decide and do everything, because they subconsciously imagine themselves as above their parishioners. The late Francis Cardinal George labeled that mindset "clericalism," a "sinful attitude," where a cleric feels "accountable only to himself and his own ideas . . . it's found in many places in the church." Well, that attitude is the last thing we need. Lucy or Samuel couldn't do what they do if their pastor had infantilized rather than empowered them.

It's "pastor, pastor, pastor," rather, in that pastors stand at the nexus of parish life, able to encourage new ideas or stifle them, willing to find and empower lay talent or quash it. Without a great pastor-partner, our Lucys and Samuels would remain, to strain for an analogy, like the talent of that gospel parable that is entrusted to the fearful servant who then buries, instead of investing, it. The wise steward-pastor, in contrast, like the parish priest in Kangemi, will be the one who sees the abundant talent that the Lord had placed at his disposal and invests it by making highest use of their gifts.

## Our New Culture of Leadership in Action

Fortunately, we have loads of great pastors. Just as the good steward in that parable turned five talents into ten, I found one pastor-leader who has managed to turn 300 into 600, in a sense. Fr. Chris Walsh serves in the Philadelphia Archdiocese. Though we New Yorkers hate just about everything that comes from there, starting with the Eagles and Philly's other mediocre sports teams, the blood of urban Irish Catholicism runs far thicker than the water of home team allegiances. So when I met Father Chris, I felt immediate kinship. In Kangemi, I was the awkward mzungu who never quite got it; in contrast, I "got" Chris. Heck, when I mentioned my Bronx neighborhood, he knew the parish I sometimes attend. He even knew which neighborhood bar serves up Guinness beer on tap and live Irish music on weekends.

But that cultural acumen didn't prepare him to pastor Philly's St. Raymond of Penafort parish, because he now serves, as he puts it, "the minority within the minority," black Catholics, a minority within America and within our church. Maybe Chris's mother was like mine: I never saw my devout Irish mother open her mouth to sing a hymn at Mass, nor did I ever hear her complain about a boring homily (God knows, we've all heard a few). But that liturgical style was not going to fly among his new community. "I ramped up my preaching style," he says, because, he chuckles a bit, "people here want to feel as if they really went to church." The same goes for the liturgical music, perhaps above all for the music: "We re-did the music program," and then he jokes again, "We started aiming for something that would feel like St. Raymond's Apostolic Pentecostal Church," referencing the exuberant worship styles of gospel choirs and Pentecostal worship.

But it's not about entertaining congregants or putting on a show. Rather, he wanted to ensure that his parishioners "are fed, and they feel like they are fed," above all fed by the Eucharist, of course, but in every other way that might draw them closer to the Lord. That vision motivated him to make other changes. But as with all good leaders, it's not for the sake of doing something different but, as he puts it, "for the sake of the mission."

And it was precisely to serve the unchanging mission that Chris engineered change. He arrived to find a community that "was deeply welcoming, with a tremendous spirit of hospitality and pride." The parishioners and his pastor predecessor, to their great credit, had struggled hard and kept their grammar school and church doors open, a great accomplishment.

But that had come at a cost: the parish had more debt than cash on hand. And the Sunday collection wasn't offsetting that deficit, much less funding new initiatives. There was another challenge: "we had 300 people attending Masses, and there weren't many young adults with children," and, as Chris put it, "If you don't hear crying, your church doesn't have a future." He and his parishioner colleagues set out to change all that, and the way they went about it previews two themes that will surface prominently later in this book—becoming more entrepreneurial and more accountable.

Chris enthusiastically experimented with new styles of liturgy, new efforts at forming disciples, new ways of managing finances, you name it. In line with Pope Francis's exhortation, Chris is not stuck with the complacent attitude of doing things the way they've always been done before. That's vital, because today's pastors typically face a plethora of challenges that cry out for innovation: Mass attendance is slipping, or weekly collections aren't supporting parish ministries, or young adults aren't showing up. Frequently, pastors face all those problems simultaneously.

What's required at such times is not the bureaucrat who runs business as usual, but the entrepreneur who will test new ways of attacking old problems. Some pastors may have been lucky enough to have inherited that scrappy entrepreneur gene. If not? I ask Chris how else he or colleagues might come by the resourcefulness to cope with change. "On the job training," he says, "and who you choose to surround yourself with." During early priestly assignments, "you look for good mentors."

Trouble is, as the priestly ranks have dwindled, many priests are thrust into pastorships very early on, before seeing many mentors in action. And the seminary curriculum, understandably steeped in theology and pastoral studies, doesn't allocate time to study project planning, marketing, driving change, or other entrepreneurial skills.

That's not necessarily a problem, if we embrace the new culture of leadership. Chances are, any pastor is preaching to a congregation filled with entrepreneurial and organizational talent. Yes, Chris Walsh struck me as having enough entrepreneurial spunk to spark a Silicon Valley high-tech start-up. But even if he totally lacked it, he could tap the leadership talent of his congregation, as that wise Kangemi pastor does.

Trouble is, we still seem to have some "worst of both worlds" pastors: they don't have entrepreneurial skills yet are unwilling to invite others to help lead. That's a deadly combination for the church. *Same Call, Different Men*, for example, explored the ways in which priests' attitudes differ from one generation to another. One of the researchers' findings is curious, and disturbing. The youngest cohort of priests is less likely than older priests to welcome leadership support from lay colleagues. For example, while 85 percent of priests ordained before or during Vatican II believe that the church "needs to move faster in empowering laypersons in ministry," only 65 percent of younger priests believe that. What's more, substantially fewer of these younger priests want to focus primarily on the parish's sacramental life while making room for greater lay responsibility in administrative areas. The mindset is deeply worrisome: add that way of thinking to the shrinking number of priests and mushrooming set of challenges, and one has an utterly unworkable formula.

Put plainly, these few misguided clerics need an attitude transplant. We face a world of challenge and opportunity, and the solution is not the solitary, beleaguered pastor who believes he will handle it without partnering with his congregants. The only way forward is the co-responsible church that Chris Walsh, that Kangemi pastor, and thousands more great priests are helping to create.

To be sure, it's not about trying things in an undisciplined fashion. Good leaders also hold themselves accountable for their actions and results. At one point during my conversation with Chris Walsh, for example, he plopped a sheaf of paper onto the table. I could see trend lines and charts; it almost resembled something from my investment banking days, and I wondered whether he was about to show me how he has invested the parish's money and ask for hot stock tips.

Hardly. He wasn't charting the stock market's progress but his parish's progress, so to speak. He uses a survey tool called the Disciple Maker Index (in a later chapter, we'll meet the Catholic Leadership Institute, the group that put together the index). As Chris and his lay colleagues innovate new worship approaches or new ministries, they are not flying blind or stubbornly sticking to their own ideological predispositions and preferences. Rather, the index gives them a way of asking parishioners some of the questions that we Catholics need to ask ourselves, questions like whether my parish "helps me to grow spiritually," or whether I would be "likely to recommend" my parish to a neighbor. Nobody can credibly lead a major organization without knowing whether things are going well or poorly; now, Chris can tell in some systematic fashion whether, for example, his parishioners feel they are growing spiritually or have plateaued.

So is it working? Well, recall that Chris Walsh inherited a parish that was averaging about 300 Sunday Mass attendees? That number has risen to 600 weekly attendees, an extraordinary result when one considers how many urban churches have closed throughout the Northeast after suffering persistently declining attendance. And remember that Chris Walsh inherited an indebted parish that was subsidized by the Archdiocese? Well, now St. Raymond is doing the subsidizing: they chip in to the Archdiocesan pool that supports other struggling ministries, this notwithstanding that St. Raymond serves a community of extremely modest means.

So what have we learned so far about the new culture of leadership?

*Everyone leads*: Our strategy will arise atop this foundational cornerstone. Organizations need to unleash all their talent when facing great challenges, when complexity renders it impossible for any handful of hierarchical leaders to respond adequately to the many and shifting problems that rear their heads. Fortunately, we are incredibly well positioned to rise to the leadership call: we're a billion-strong church that has been blessed with every conceivable talent.

We earlier quoted the Vatican Secretary of State's reference to a "sacramental emergency" that is already emerging here and there, and we can all pray for vocations and for the Holy Spirit's guidance as the Pope and bishops discern how to make the sacraments sufficiently available to all Catholics.

But another grave emergency is also upon us: call it a "leadership emergency," and every one of us plays a role in addressing it. A Church of one billion persons and more than 200,000 parishes will not be revitalized by the actions of a Pope and some 200 Cardinals. Rather, revitalization will happen only when a critical mass of engaged Catholics step up and lead.

Think of it this way: we're all already leading *anyway*, well or poorly. Recall that dictionary definition: we are all "pointing out the way and influencing others." Every day, in small or large ways, my values and behaviors are "pointing out the way" of Jesus (or not) and influencing those around me, who may be thinking: *hmm, I want some of what she seems to have*, or, alternatively, *yuck; if that's how these Catholics behave, I'm not missing anything by sleeping in on Sunday.*

But beyond this everyday leadership, the real leap forward occurs when we don't see ourselves as passive participants in church but as co-responsible leaders of the church. That will entail a huge mindset shift for us. Take, in contrast, New York's thriving Redeemer Presbyterian Church, whose senior pastor, Tim Keller, talks about "half the attendance . . . involved in some kind of ministry," and who encourages the flock to think of themselves as "lay ministers" for starters, and then even as "leaders of leaders, people who are . . . mentors and supervisors to newer lay leaders." Or take Chicagoland's burgeoning Willow Creek church, where 1,000 volunteers step up weekly to power the congregation's many works of prayer, service, or outreach.

Imagine the power that will be unleashed when half of all Catholics start taking more ownership of their respective parishes, even thinking of themselves as "leaders of leaders." Imagine what our larger parishes will become with fully 1,000 volunteers each week involved in one or another ministry or task. Now, I suspect a few readers are thinking: *we don't even need 1,000 volunteers to keep our parish running. It's running okay now.* That's just it. It's not about "keeping the parish running" as it runs now. It's about imagining whole new ways of being a parish and a global church in order to meet the many challenges highlighted earlier. What new roles, methods, ministries, or approaches will emerge when more and more of us start stepping up to lead? I'm confident that all kinds of ideas will blossom as soon as we start fostering a new culture of leadership and are called to lead by pastors, bishops, and others.

From there, two further commonsense axioms follow, as discussed below.

## No Changed Outcomes without Changed Approaches

*The urgency of changed approaches for changed outcomes:* When things are going poorly, they rarely improve by doing more of what spawned the poor results in the first place. For that reason, we all must become change agents. It's arduous to galvanize a commitment to change in a large institution, above all in our venerable church, where we have grown understandably wedded to familiar ways of doing things. But complacency is insidious when things are not going well. Think, for example, of all the opportunities we are missing, starting with our own young adult children who find the church irrelevant, our neighbors who drifted away because the parish offers scant spiritual nourishment, or the marginalized folks who never even get our attention. These lost "opportunities" are people, and their absence from our midst is a silent scream for us to lead the changes that might bring better outcomes.

## A ONE-TEAM MINDSET: UNITING THE CHURCH (FINALLY)

But change *what*? Chances are, the preceding paragraphs angered many readers. Some may have thought: become change agents? The misguided changes after Vatican II are what got us into this mess. While others surely thought exactly the opposite: the misguided reluctance to follow through on Vatican II's vision is what got us into this mess—three decades of near paralysis and slow decline. Just about everyone would champion some kind of change or reform, but the changes that might delight one Catholic tribe may dismay another. Such divisions are our church's agony.

That's not how great organizations stay great. Rather, they manage to coalesce around some higher viewpoint. As a wise leader once put it: "the higher the calling, the higher the compelling vision that you can articulate, then the more it pulls everybody in." It wasn't a bishop who articulated that plainly spiritual wisdom; rather, it was Alan Mulally, then chief executive of Ford Motor Company. One of a leader's prime tasks is to lift us above our own narrow viewpoints to unite us around some higher calling, in this case the overarching mission of revitalizing the church we love. The time comes for organizations to stop dissipating their energies in internecine strife and to rally around goals that can unite them.

That has not happened for us, and it's long overdue. We're stuck, and we have to get ourselves unstuck through a compelling common vision and strategy that draws everyone in. Thankfully, our compelling vision already exists and always has: the person of Jesus. "Everyone leads" will be a vital key to our church's future, but only if everyone leads in the way that Jesus points. For that reason, we now to turn to Jesus and remind ourselves of Jesus's leadership style, approach, and values.

## *Pray, Reflect, Discuss, and Act*

- For all of us: Reflect on your call to leadership. Pray over (and/ or discuss with a group) Benedict XVI's call to "co-responsibility": what does that mean to you? In what ways could you show greater "co-responsibility"?

- Discuss (in your parish or diocese): what are three completely new ways in which we can tap the leadership gifts and talents of our congregants and/or staff, not by piling more tasks on their already over-burdened shoulders but by greater participation in brainstorming, decision-making, or strategy-setting.

- For pastors and bishops: Apprise congregants of the local church's challenges and call them to help lead.

- For Catholic universities or dioceses: Convene a "Theology of Leadership" conference to develop deeper insight on the leadership implications of the baptismal call or, for example, of Benedict XVI's call to "co-responsibility."

# CHAPTER FOUR

# Follow the Leaders

## *Rediscovering Jesus and the Early Christians*

POINT YOUR FINGER AT THE MOON TONIGHT, AND REMIND YOURSELF why the church differs from any worldly institution. That little ritual reminded me what this chapter is about and what our church is about. We are in the "business" of pointing to the moon, and whenever we forget it, we get into trouble.

I thank Archbishop Georg Gänswein for the image. He might be the most famous guy that his fellow Catholics don't know. Tens of millions of us have seen him often, yet few even know his name. But just type "Pope Benedict and Gänswein" or "Pope Francis and Gänswein" into an internet search engine, and you can kill an afternoon browsing through photos of Gänswein as Prefect of the Papal Household, handing documents to the Pope or sitting beside him in the Popemobile. (Not that Gänswein is some lightweight lackey. He is a canon lawyer and published author.)

Curious reporters imagined that this living link between two popes must have interesting secrets to share. Perhaps an enterprising reporter might pry a little gossip from the trusted aide-de-camp? Did Benedict approve of how Francis was leading the church?

The Archbishop's answer to such questions? As he told one interviewer: it's not about the pope. Rather, each pope was like a finger pointing to the moon, the moon being a metaphorical allusion to God. "Sometimes this gets turned upside down," Gänswein said, "and all people see is the finger—they don't see the moon."

It's not about the pope; it's about the moon (God). So too for the church—it's not about us, it's about God. And the way we Christians point to God is through Jesus: "I am the way, the truth, and the life," Jesus told us, and "no one comes to the Father except through me" (John 14:6).

That reality renders us radically different from every business on earth. I long worked in an investment bank that, like Christianity, was named after its legendary founder—in that case, J. P. Morgan. But whereas our church exists to lead people to a personal relationship with Jesus, our investment bank was not about facilitating encounters with J. P. Morgan's ghost. Rather, we existed to win business for our firm, and we hoped to earn a boatload of money by doing so. To a large extent, it really was about us.

But we go badly astray as a church whenever it becomes about us, or about a pope, the Vatican, our institution's prerogatives, our financial affairs, protecting the institution's reputation when scandals emerge, erecting impressive buildings, or anything like that. We've seen, to our agony and shame, what happens when we start focusing on the institution instead of Jesus. When testifying about the Australian church hierarchy's dreadful mishandling of pedophilia, Cardinal George Pell attributed it to an instinct "to protect the institution, the community of the church, from shame." They had it backward, as did too many shepherds in the United States, Ireland, Belgium, Germany, the Netherlands, and, sadly, too many other countries. Jesus, our unchanging center, comes first, not the institution.

We point to the moon, or, as Pope John Paul II once put it, our mission, "has its centre in Christ himself, who is to be known, loved and imitated.... This programme for all times is our programme for the Third Millennium."

Jesus is the touchstone for all else in this book. What are our strategic priorities? Jesus's priorities. This chapter accordingly centers us on Jesus as prelude to all that will follow. Good strategies typically drive needed change, but great strategies are always anchored in something unchanging, an orienting North Star that keeps us on course. Our strategic North Star is Jesus.

Our church may have lost track of its North Star, at least a bit. I wouldn't dare render so harsh a judgment, but prominent bishops did so in the closing report of their synod on the New Evangelization, a few years ago. They said that the Church, "feels the need to sit beside today's men and women. She wants to render the Lord present in their lives . . . presenting once more the beauty and perennial newness of the encounter with Christ to the often distracted and confused heart and mind of the men and women of our time."

## TIME TO "REDISCOVER" THE WAY OF JESUS

Distracted and confused indeed. So many men and women are increasingly distanced from Catholicism and increasingly entranced by shopping, social media, money, sex, and dozens more contemporary charms. I wondered how exactly we might successfully present, "the beauty and perennial newness of the encounter with Christ" with greater success than is currently being attained.

The bishops had an answer: "We need to rediscover the ways in which Jesus approached persons and called them, in order to put these approaches into practice in today's circumstances." That answer enthused me: it seemed so obvious and so right.

So I set out to rediscover the way of Jesus. My wife and I pray together each morning, before the maelstrom of e-mails, phone calls, and to-do lists claims our attention. We offer the petitions that weigh on our respective hearts, pray the Our Father, and read the day's gospel. How better to "rediscover the way of Jesus" than to read his words and the stories remembered by those who knew him? Sure, I had lots of opinions about Jesus after attending Catholic schools and hearing hundreds of homilies. But that may have been precisely the problem that the synod bishops were getting at: yes, we are all pretty sure that we know Jesus, so well that everything Jesus says and does seems to fit each of our long-settled ideas about his way and priorities.

So instead of relying on my preconceptions and picking gospel stories that would subtly amplify the points I intended to make in this book, I would metaphorically accompany Jesus, trying to listen as if hearing him for the very first time.

On the day I started, Jesus encountered various disease sufferers, and "he laid his hands on each of them and cured them" (Luke 4:40). He then left for other towns, to "proclaim the good news of the Kingdom of God . . . because for this purpose I have been sent" (Luke 4:43). It's been estimated that fully 700 of the gospel's 3,700 verses somehow involve healing accounts, and they started to blur and lose impact until I imagined what stir would erupt if a stranger wandered into midtown Manhattan and performed such feats. A guy in a Statue of Liberty costume can attract a crowd in Manhattan; a guy who heals withered limbs at the intersection of Broadway and 42nd Street? Fuhgeddaboutit, as we say. Pandemonium. Even a reality television show, if he wanted one.

## "No One Would Be So Brutal"

Soon after came a set of passages that remain "ever ancient and ever new," to borrow St. Augustine's phrase. Multitudes gathered around Jesus, Luke tells us, "And all the crowd sought to touch him, for power came forth from him and healed them all" (Luke 6:19). A long, extended teaching passage follows, as if Jesus is laying out his vision, or, in John Paul II's words, "the programme for all times."

Jesus pronounces as "blessed" all those who are, "poor . . . that hunger . . . or that weep" (Luke 6:21). Jesus instructs us to, "Love your enemies, do good to those who hate you . . . and pray for those who abuse you . . . Give to everyone who begs from you" (Luke 6: 27–28, 30). Do good to those who hate you? Give to *everyone* who begs? I wondered whether these radical instructions shocked Jesus's listeners as thoroughly as they now shock me. Worldly logic wants only the worst for our enemies, but "Jesus logic" calls us to love and do good for them. Indeed, compared to such bracing commands, the golden rule sounds almost tame: "And as you wish that men would do to you, do so to them."

We Christians will surely fascinate the world once more when we live those commands so thoroughly that they became our global "brand," so to speak—the very first thing that comes to an outsider's mind upon hearing the word "Christian." Centuries ago, St. John Chrysostom imagined the impact that our witness might have: "There would be no Heathen, if we were such Christians as we ought to be. If we kept the commandments of Christ, if we suffered injury, if we allowed advantage to be taken of us, if being reviled we blessed, if being ill-treated we did good, if this were the general practice among us, no one would be so brutal as not to become a convert to godliness."

This must be why the bishops encouraged themselves and the rest of us to "rediscover" the way in which Jesus approached persons. He so often introduced himself through deeds of mercy. Is that how we introduce ourselves to the world today? He heals indiscriminately, not as part of a proposed transaction: he doesn't ask first whether those he helps have already reformed their lives or will become his disciples. Yet, so often, those whom he encounters are transformed—they become grateful people; they praise God; they want to share the good news. Even the outwardly healthy are transformed by encountering Jesus, like those fishermen who, against all logic, leave behind their nets to follow him.

He reaches out constantly, rarely to the well-respected and often, to put it indelicately, to society's misfits and losers: lepers, Samaritans, tax collectors, prostitutes, menial laborers, and, above all, to the impoverished. Indeed, his leadership team includes social outcasts or poorly educated sorts who would never be considered suitable candidates for a bishop's office nowadays. And, like the poor people he serves, Jesus himself lives simply, with no apparent headquarters, means of support, or possessions.

Church-calendar aficionados could pinpoint my "rediscover Jesus project" to September 2015, when the preceding string of passages from St. Luke comprised the daily Mass gospels. As I read, I was consoled to think that millions more Catholics, from Johannesburg to Seattle, were reading the same passages. The power of this shared tradition cannot be overestimated. We Catholics represent every culture and nation on earth. Yet, as we discern our shared path through this confusing century, we start with the same Lord and share the same vision and values.

Leaders, the last chapter stressed, "point the way and influence others," and Jesus's "way" of approaching humanity is so inspiring and clear that the preliminary contours of our "EASTeR Project" already begin to draw into focus. Like Jesus, we will especially direct our energies toward all those who are marginalized in society, whether through poverty or otherwise: we will serve all in need. As the late Francis Cardinal George once put it, "We are part of a kingdom where the poor are the favored sons and daughters."

And we will not sit back and wait for the world to find its way to our doorstep, but reach out to engage and welcome others, like Jesus who was always on the move, "to visit other towns and proclaim the Good News." And the world will recognize us as the Lord's disciples by our witness to the greatest of his commandments, namely that we love God with our whole heart and soul, and love our neighbors as we love ourselves. Our challenge, then, is not to figure out Jesus's values but simply to role model "Jesus logic" more thoroughly, in ways that will once again fascinate our own children and the world at large.

But an irony arises. Though Jesus has fascinated the world for centuries, he frankly failed to fascinate many during his lifetime. As his earthly life ended, he had gathered only a few handfuls of frightened followers, virtually all of whom deserted him during his hours of need. Yet, despite that unpromising track record, he is audacious enough, in his final post-Resurrection appearance, to articulate a mission of breathtaking scope: "go and make disciples of all nations." Then he ascends to heaven. In many artistic renderings of the moment, the Apostles look up in open-mouthed wonder, stupefied at this Jesus who has risen from the dead and who now floats off into heaven.

But one might playfully, if irreverently, imagine other reasons for stupefaction: "Hey, Lord, only now you get around to telling us about making disciples of all nations? We're a small bunch of Jews who have been wandering a small patch of Galilee. You yourself failed to gather many disciples. And now at the last minute you drop this multinational mission into our laps?"

How are they supposed to do that? Any competent chief executive would have articulated the broad outlines of a strategy and built an organization to support it. Sure, some visionaries are "big picture" folks who entrust the details to subordinates. But Jesus entrusts to followers even fundamental questions that will determine the church's very identity and future: Should non-Jews be included in the Jesus movement, for example? Should the followers of Jesus continue to adhere to the strictures of Jewish law?

And it's not as if Jesus entrusted these church-shaping decisions to apostles who inspire great confidence. At one point, two of them angle for prime seats in heaven, under the wrongheaded impression that Jesus's Kingdom revolves around power and status, like worldly kingdoms. One of his leadership team betrays him to death; another denies knowing him during the passion.

Let's face it: either Jesus was incompetent when it came to establishing an institutional church, or Jesus was primarily dedicated to establishing something more fundamental: the Kingdom's eternal values and the way to the Father. The old cliché has some truth: Jesus didn't set out to create an institutional church that happens to have a mission; he created a mission that happens to have a church. That mission? Well, in Gänswein's shorthand: to point to the moon, to invite others to a transforming encounter with God in Jesus. The heart of our mission is not a church building but a person: Jesus. The Eucharist is called the "source" and center of Catholic life because Jesus is the source and center of Catholic life.

Every generation ever since, from the Apostles to ourselves, has had to figure out how to incarnate that mission in its historical circumstances: how to change, renew, or reform an institutional church that is stewarded by flawed humans, so that we can better serve what is unchanging and unflawed: the mission and values that Jesus gave us. Jesus left no organization chart, manual of operating procedures, or even the rudiments of a strategy. He promised only to send the Holy Spirit.

And so we find ourselves today, metaphorically like that first generation of apostles huddled in that upper room. Jesus had missioned them to make disciples of all nations, and they hadn't a clue how to get started. And our current predicament is not entirely dissimilar, for, as an earlier chapter made painfully clear, we don't quite know how to make disciples either, in many ways. We know how to "inherit" those who are born into our community, but have proven less adept at winning the interest of postmodern men and women, or young adults, or those who feel alienated by church teachings, among countless others.

The early apostles were afraid to leave their upper room, and we're pretty stuck in our own metaphorical upper rooms, talking to each other or talking at the world instead of engaging it. Those disciples were in every way a cultural minority; their beliefs were little known and insignificant in Rome's great empire. And while one could hardly call Christianity insignificant nowadays, a growing population see us as antiquated and irrelevant to their lives and well-being.

## First-Century Lessons for Twenty-First-Century Leaders

If the early apostles' challenge is a metaphor for ours, perhaps we can learn from them. Indeed, the more I reread the Acts and the New Testament letters, the more convinced I became that too many of us Catholic Christians are looking to the wrong era. Some of us may wish it were the late 1960s again, just after Vatican II, as we see it, had opened a fresh new world; or the late 1950s again, just before Vatican II, to our way of thinking, ushered in chaos; or, we may envision a world like the late medieval era, when Catholicism wielded virtually unchallenged cultural hegemony over the lives of Christians.

But let's look further back and learn four first-century lessons for revitalizing our twenty-first-century church: first, let's call the Spirit into our midst; second, let's show leadership like Lucius, Gaius, Lydia, Silas, Priscilla, Aquila, Phoebe the deacon, and other unsung heroes like them; third, let's go to the metaphorical equivalent of Derbe, Lystra, Berea, Troas, and further afield; and fourth, let's balance change and continuity. The balance of this chapter will illuminate those four opaque-sounding lessons.

### First: Call God's Spirit into Our Midst

After Jesus had ascended, the disciples huddled in an upper room and prayed fervently, hunkering down for as long as ten days or more. One might wonder: left to their own devices, would they ever have left that room and attempted the mission that Jesus had given them?

Well, two billion people call themselves Christians today because the apostles were not left to their own devices. Their lives were transformed when "a sound came from heaven like the rush of a mighty wind . . . and there appeared to them tongues as of fire, distributed and resting on each one of them" (Acts 1:2). The writer Tom Cahill coined the term "hinges of history," referring to those inflection points when civilization's arc has turned powerfully in some promising new direction. Pentecost is a hinge of our church history. Before it, Jesus's followers are, for the most part, unsure, unimaginative, and frightened.

They emerge from Pentecost as if flung by centrifugal force. They scatter in all directions and plant new faith communities. They conceive revolutionary new ideas about accepting non-Jews into the Jesus movement, ideas that would have been inconceivable and unacceptable to them months earlier. Decades ago, Pope John Paul II pleaded that we approach our mission with "new methods, new expressions, and new ardor." He might as well have said, "Hey, we need to get our first-century mojo back." We need to start drinking some of what those men and women in Acts were drinking.

What they were imbibing was God's Holy Spirit. Yes, we need to rediscover the ways of Jesus if we are to succeed in this new century. But we likewise need to rediscover God's Holy Spirit, the wellspring for the courage, imagination, and resourcefulness that we now sorely need. As a good Catholic boy, I long ago learned about the Holy Spirit's seven gifts, such as understanding, counsel, and piety. But upon a closer reading of Acts, such sober words feel too tame, as if we are trying to cage the Holy Spirit within our own sterile intellectual categories.

Drink in that spirit through a few representative passages: "[They] spoke the word of God with boldness" (Acts 4:31), and "when they saw the boldness of Peter and John, and perceived that they were uneducated, common men, they were astonished" (Acts 4:13), and "I am acting with great boldness toward you . . . In all our affliction, I am overflowing with joy" (2 Cor. 7:4), and, well, you get the idea. What's striking is not just how often such allusions to boldness show up in Acts or in Paul's or other epistles, but how seldom similar ideas crop up in pre-Pentecost descriptions of Jesus's followers.

These men and women were transformed by God's Spirit. They have embraced their call to lead, now courageous enough to drive change and pursue their goals with appropriate urgency. The previous chapter used the image of "unleashing" each person's leadership potential, and now that idea takes clearer shape. In one respect, those in hierarchical authority, whether in our church or in any other organization, are accountable for "unleashing" the leadership potential of their teams by inviting others to use their gifts fully and creating meaningful opportunities for that to happen.

But complementary to this organizational empowerment is the Holy Spirit's power to unleash courage, imagination, and ardor. As these innovative heroes of Acts are leading, they are described as "led by the spirit" or "following the Spirit." Thus they validate another aspect of our Christian vision of leadership: we are all leaders *and* followers.

Thus our ancestors' first lesson to us: without God's Spirit blowing through our community, our strategies will be nothing more than so much hot air. Like every organization, we need inspired leadership, but we Christians believe that authentic leadership is quite literally "inspired," a word derived from the Latin *inspirare*, meaning to breathe or blow into. When worldly organizations want to turn people into better leaders, they give them books or send them to workshops. When we Christians want to turn ourselves or others into better leaders, we must likewise avail ourselves of the best formation and training out there, as we role model the professionalism and excellence that befits a shining city on a hill. But we do something else as well: call upon God's Holy Spirit to inspire us, to "breathe" the Spirit's gifts into our hearts.

### Second: Bottom-Up Leadership, from Everyone

Which gets to a second encouraging lesson from these early Christians: any one of us can become an inspired leader. Don't take my word for it; read Acts, which validates our new culture of leadership, where everyone leads. The Jesus of John's gospel says of the Spirit, "the wind blows where it wills, and you do not know whence it comes or wither it goes" (John 3:8). So it is in Acts. One unheralded Christian after another steps up to make some vital leadership contribution. As I read the chapters, I often thought: *Who are all these people?* Who are these characters like Priscilla, Erastus, or others who pop up in one or another chapter and contribute instrumentally to the fledgling church's growth or success? A need becomes apparent, and someone steps up to show initiative, exactly the leadership mentality we want to cultivate.

As a young boy, I had assumed that the Acts of the Apostles was about, well, the twelve Apostles. In time, I appreciated that many of the twelve go virtually unmentioned in Acts, and, as one interested in the church's revitalization, I read Acts differently. Yes, it's the story of Paul, Timothy, Stephen, and other well-known figures. But Acts is equally a story of unsung heroes who had never walked alongside Jesus, were likely not in the upper room on the Pentecost, had not been trained for leadership, yet nonetheless played crucial roles. They had no catechism, New Testament, or creed to guide them: if they could seize their leadership moment in those circumstances, surely we can do so in ours, with all the resources at our disposal.

### Third: The Action Is at the Frontiers, Not "Headquarters"

It's not just who shows leadership in Acts, but where they show it. Yes, crucial episodes transpire at the Jesus movement's Jerusalem "headquarters." Decisions are taken there that have determined the church's course ever since. Still, the real action is not at headquarters but in countless other locales where enterprising disciples spread the Good News. We all know frontiers like Ephesus or Corinth, thanks to the titles of Paul's letters. But that's merely the highlight tour; the full itinerary includes Lystra, Derbe, Athens, and plenty more.

Thus their third lesson to us: the action is at the frontiers. Crummy organizations are centripetal: that is, they suck energy, resources, and attention to the center. Headquarters is the black hole where initiatives and ideas are swallowed and die. Great organizations are instead centrifugal: they radiate energy forth from headquarters to every corner of the organization's world. The center serves those in the field, not the other way around.

We contemporary Catholics are too often watching what happens in Rome, when our future is being won or lost elsewhere. Reams of ink (and its cyber-equivalent) have chronicled the dysfunctional Vatican curia or poorly governed Vatican bank. Sure, high-quality stewardship of money and resources must become a hallmark if we hope to speak credibly to the modern world. But let's face it: those who have deserted Catholicism did not leave because the Vatican bank was a mess, and they're not coming back just because it gets fixed.

Rather, hearts and minds will be won at the frontiers, just as for our ancestors. But there's a big difference between then and now. Their frontiers were often geographic, as the fledgling Jesus movement ventured a hundred and then a thousand miles beyond its Jerusalem base.

But our new frontiers have little to do with geography. The new frontier is not a faraway country but in our community, hidden in plain sight: the homeless, refugees, infirm elderly, or mentally unstable to whom we do not reach out. The new frontier is right in our family: the adolescent and young adult children who find us judgmental or irrelevant. Paul and colleagues knew the obvious—the only way to reach frontiers like Ephesus was to go there. We have to relearn the obvious: we also have to "go there," whether to the young adults, religious skeptics, homeless, or those whose sexuality or marital status marginalizes them from our teaching. Jesus and the early Christians ventured forth to the frontiers; how naïve, arrogant, or lazy it would be for us today to presume that those on our frontiers should instead find their own way to our doorstep.

### Fourth: Balancing Change and Continuity
And we'll have to be as resourceful on our new frontiers as early Christians were on theirs. They figured out how to convey their message to those who didn't speak their language or think about the world as they did. We too have to convey our message in unfamiliar territories: among those who want to make their own decisions about personal morality, don't see what value our faith holds for their lives, or who consider us an anachronistic dinosaur of an institution. Our forebears realized that they would have to proclaim their message in new ways to have it heard; we don't yet get that. The apostle Paul, in describing his approach to ministry, exemplified the adaptable spirit that we must rediscover: "to those under the law I became as one under the law," and "to those outside the law I became as one outside the law," and "to the weak, I became weak . . . I have become all things to all men . . . I do it all for the sake of the gospel" (1 Cor. 9: 22–23).

Paul's lyric phrasing may make it sound easy. It wasn't: the early church was racked by inharmonious debates over change. For example, could a non-Jew become Christian without first converting to Judaism? Paul argued for a more expansive church. Others plausibly argued that Jesus would have wanted no such thing: didn't Jesus once state that his ministry was intended only for Jews: "I was sent only to the lost sheep of the house of Israel"? (Matt. 15:24)

Yet here was Paul, not only welcoming Gentile converts but dispensing them from the requirements of Jewish law like circumcision. When the apostle Peter eventually waded into the controversy, Paul confronted him, "I opposed [Peter] to his face, because he stood condemned" (Gal. 2:11), adding that Peter, "had not been straightforward about the truth of the gospel" (Gal. 2:14). Ouch. Imagine a bishop hurling such an accusation into the Pope's face today, in public no less.

Well, all of us uncircumcised Gentile Christians know how the early church resolved that question. But the point is not circumcision, rather, more generally, the vast breadth of change that these early leaders boldly engineered, abandoning rituals that Jesus himself would have held holy.

We Catholics have a great grasp of our tradition but little sense of our history, it's sometimes said. Our history confronts us with a profound paradox: the willingness to adapt is not a departure from our tradition but fundamentally part of our tradition. So much that we nowadays revere as "timeless tradition" is, in fact, the result of change.

Just think, for example, of our tradition's most exalted moment, when the priest recounts Jesus's words from the Last Supper and we partake of the Eucharist, just as the apostles did. Yet so many of the rituals surrounding this solemn moment have nothing to do with that Last Supper. A priest's vestments resemble a Roman senator's dress and nothing worn by Jesus or the twelve. I don't attend Mass in someone's home, as the earliest Christians did; rather, I attend Mass in an oblong church, with the altar situated in a semicircular apse, an architectural shape that any pagan Roman would have recognized as a basilica, a meeting hall.

I would be scandalized today to attend Mass and discover that dinner was also being served in the sanctuary, yet my earliest Christian ancestors might well have been just as scandalized by the absence of a meal. They would have been mystified to find me on my knees during the consecration, as I am mildly offended when able-bodied Christians sit during that same moment.

Second-century Justin Martyr bequeathed us one of the earliest extended accounts of the Mass, and his words make clear both how much has changed, and how much hasn't. The community gathered together, he tells us, offered up prayers of petition, exchanged a sign of peace, offered the bread and wine, heard readings from sacred scripture, and received the Eucharist. Every Mass, from Argentina to Alaska, still incorporates these moments.

But much else within the Mass evolved over centuries. These changes distance me from the historical Jesus yet draw me closer to the living Jesus. I'm grateful that the Our Father and Sanctus were eventually added to the Mass, and for bells at the consecration, that I kneel at solemn moments, and that I'm encouraged to receive communion more frequently than once a year.

Am I suggesting that the Mass is a hodgepodge that can be revised on a whim? Of course not. But if we Catholic Christians are to revere our tradition, we must embrace it fully, and it has been living rather than ossified.

## EMBRACE THE BEST PRACTICES WE CAN FIND
We inherit the legacy of innovative ancestors, who accommodated us uncircumcised Gentiles, reframed their beliefs into language that would engage Greek intellectual culture, and who adapted the Roman Empire's vernacular as their church's lingua franca. What's more, our ancestors freely adopted secular society's most advanced administrative practices from the Roman Empire. It's from Rome, for example, that we came by a system of dioceses and vicariates.

Well, the Romans weren't the last civilization to develop good ideas for organizing and running institutions. I suspect our ancestors would encourage us to do exactly as they did: embrace the best administrative and managerial practices that the world can offer.

None of this is about reckless experimentation, though, which gets to a challenge that confronts every organization, and above all our church: what should change, and what should not? That question is bedeviling us, just as debates over circumcision tore at those early Christians. We'll get through our debates by recalling Paul's standard: "I have become all things to all men . . . I do it all for the sake of the gospel." The apostle, on the one hand, declares his radical openness to change, his readiness, "to become all things." Yet at the same time, he articulates the criterion for distinguishing worthy changes from misguided ones: is this proposed change aligned with gospel truth, that is, is it, "for the sake of the gospel"?

Paul's guidance uncannily anticipates a wise modern mantra, namely that successful organizations, "preserve the core, and stimulate progress." The phrase was coined by two Stanford University professors whose research had compared highly successful companies against mediocre also-rans. They noticed that successful companies typically manifest a creative tension. On the one hand, they were unflinchingly devoted to some non-negotiables, like their sense of mission, core values, or devotion to a customer base. They zealously preserved their core but, on the other hand, would willingly change just about anything else in order to serve the core mission more effectively.

Preserve the core and stimulate progress: that creative tension keeps organizations anchored but prevents them from becoming stuck. They are rooted, but keep growing. They move forward rapidly, but never lose track of where they come from. In fact, it's precisely their secure identity that enables them to move confidently, even boldly, in new directions. Mediocre organizations, in contrast, never get that creative balance right. Some seem to lack any core; subject to whims or fads, they drift. They lack the firm standards against which to judge one proposed change worthy and another one wrongheaded.

Other organizations, conversely, doom themselves through the opposite instinct: virtually no change is acceptable; every cow is sacred; no risk is worth taking; every innovative idea seems a threat to "the ways we've always done it around here." Because they cannot adapt, the world leaves them behind. They stagnate.

## Drink More Deeply from Our Own Wells

We face great challenges, but our living tradition blesses us with all the resources we need to rebuild our church. All we need do is drink more deeply from our own wells. We will rediscover the ways in which Jesus approached persons. And we will embrace the innovative leadership style of our early Christian ancestors in order to accomplish our mission effectively in this complex, changing world. We now outline a strategy to do so, an EASTeR project to build a thriving, twenty-first-century church.

## *Pray, Reflect, Discuss, and Act*

- Read and pray over one of the synoptic gospels, individually or in prayer groups. As you "rediscover" the way of Jesus, what seems relevant to our task of revitalizing our church?

- Pray regularly for God's Holy Spirit to bring a new Pentecost for the church's revitalization.

- Discuss: For the apostles, the frontiers were both geographic and cultural, as they encountered the Gentile world beyond Judaea: what are the new "frontiers" for your parish or ministry?

- Discuss: How does our church's culture, our habitual ways of thinking and operating, seem similar or different to that of our early Christian ancestors? What should we learn from them as we revitalize the church?

CHAPTER FIVE

# The EASTeR Project

## *A Strategy That Can Revitalize Our Church*

WE CATHOLICS ARE AN EASTER PEOPLE, AND WE WILL REVITALIZE OUR church through an EASTeR strategy.

That unexplained acronym may initially leave readers lost, and, not coincidentally, this chapter begins with a few lost soldiers. They will illustrate one of a good strategy's benefits and invite us to gratitude for the church's riches. By chapter's end, we will have mapped a strategy that calls every one of us to lead our church where it needs to go.

I've more than once flown over the Alps as an airline passenger, and the majestic peaks invariably tingle my spine, especially on sunny days when white snowcaps are offset by deep blue skies, and I'm transported into a welcome solitude.

Welcome solitude when beheld from an airplane seat, but what if I were dropped into the Alpine wilderness during a snowstorm? Would I be brave enough to struggle forward through thin air, or, after a few hopeless steps, lie down to die? That's more or less the choice, we're told, that confronted a small military platoon during World War I. Dispatched on a short scouting mission into Alpine terrain, they were caught by an unpredicted snowstorm that raged for two days; they were lost, freezing, terrified, and lacking just about everything needed to survive.

Everything, that is, except a map. Not that they could readily situate themselves. Lost tourists in Manhattan can orient themselves by street signs on every corner, but the Alps aren't signposted. The soldiers knew they were on a mountain, just like mountains that stretched in every direction. Still, even though they could not precisely pinpoint their starting point, the map's promise of a way forward boosted their confidence. They guessed at their coordinates and headed in the direction that seemed most viable. They encountered obstacles and dead ends, adjusted their route along the way, and eventually made it to safety.

The story lives on today mostly because of its ironic punch line. That map that helped those soldiers out of the Alps? It wasn't a map of the Alps; it was a map of the Pyrenees, a fact that only became apparent to them after they reached safety. The story, repeated by business school professors like Karl Weick, metaphorically encapsulates a crucial benefit of a strategy—it gets us going. Strategy gives us common objectives, a shared sense of direction, and plots our first few steps.

And then? If we discover that we're heading in the right direction, we speed up. But more likely, we start running into obstacles and work around them, like those soldiers. Frequently enough, we run into obstacles not because the strategy was bad, but because no one could have foreseen every challenge that would arise along the complex path to an ambitious goal. Only by venturing forth can we see the obstacles and possibilities clearly. As we journey, our problem-solving skills sharpen and confidence rises as we become more adept at conquering challenges; our vision becomes acute: we can distinguish the dead ends from more promising pathways.

## An Unexpected Key to Great Strategy: Humility
When navigating complex challenges, whether those soldiers in the Alps or a church in a secular century, the winning path is not immediately apparent. There's too much we don't know and won't discover until we venture forth, test ideas, track results, replicate successes, and learn from the inevitable failures, all the while adapting as we go. Only humble leaders can succeed, those who readily admit that they don't have the answers and who willingly learn from everyone, above all from their own subordinates and colleagues.

I learned that the hard way. I was once placed in charge of a department hobbled by inefficient operations. I studied the morass, conceived a new approach, and led my hundred-strong team forward with my best managing director swagger. Led them in the wrong direction, as it turned out. But then something curious happened. Subordinates started speaking up; folks brainstormed fixes that had never occurred to them before; others voiced ideas that they had been too intimidated to mention previously. Through collaborative effort, we ended up fixing the mess that I had inherited.

So how had I contributed to the progress? My own proposed solution had been wrongheaded. But in retrospect, I saw that it broke a logjam of sorts. Like that Pyrenees map, it got my team going. I had set a clear objective, which unified us around a common goal. I had made change an imperative—we would no longer drift along and settle for dysfunctional mediocrity. And, paradoxically, it also helped that I had been wrong; that seemed to embolden subordinates to offer their own suggestions: "heck," they may have thought, "our ideas might be wrong, but no more wrong than Chris was."

I was reminded of James Yorke, the distinguished mathematician and cofounder of chaos theory, who once quipped, "the most successful people I know are those who are good at Plan B." I had forgotten that wisdom when I started researching this book. I had digested and prayed over the statistics, becoming completely convinced that we need new strategies. We can't keep going like this. We owe it to ourselves and to the Lord to try to lift the church onto a more promising trajectory.

But change *what*? The data on what's going wrong is plentiful; the data on what will work better is not. We can demonstrate statistically that young adult interest in Catholicism is rapidly waning, that Europeans are drifting from the church, that Catholicism is not as appealing as Pentecostal churches to many in the developing world. But how do we solve these challenges? The research doesn't pinpoint one or two master solutions that will reverse these trends.

I was intimidated in other ways. Our worldwide church needs a unifying strategy, but after biting off that global chunk of a problem, I was choking on it. What could I possibly propose that would be equally meaningful in the highly secularized Netherlands, where churches are closing rapidly, and in the deeply religious Congo, where dioceses can't build churches fast enough?

Such challenges paralyzed me, until my eureka moment dawned, or, more accurately, my head-slapping "duh" moment: the most successful people I know are those who are good at Plan B. Why had I ever imagined that it would be different for the church than for every other organization forced to navigate this complex century? Why expect that the church, for example, can right away master the elusive art of engaging tech-savvy teenagers when not even Silicon Valley social media hotshots can confidently predict which apps will catch on?

That realization was liberating. I no longer felt the pressure to concoct the winning strategy and instead accepted that this book's proposals will surely be imperfect, just like strategic proposals in every industry. But once the strategic discussion is under way, my talented fellow Catholics will compensate for my shortcomings by offering their own ideas. With that shift in mindset, I began focusing on the manifold advantages the church brings to strategy-setting. We've already seen, for example, that humility is characteristic of great strategists. It disposes leaders to learn from team members and to be led by facts rather than their own ideological predispositions. They willingly admit mistakes and abandon failed strategies when appropriate, rather than arrogantly clinging to misguided approaches.

Such humility doesn't come naturally in large corporations, where competitive executives strive to project mastery; but in contrast, humility is one of our faith's core values. We say with Paul, "I will not boast, except of my weaknesses" (2 Cor. 12:5). We believe in the same message that Paul heard from God: "My grace is sufficient for you, for my power is made perfect in weakness" (2 Cor. 12:9). We're theologically disposed toward strategic humility. It would verge on blasphemy to suggest that our own wits will suffice, as if telling the Holy Spirit: *hey, I've got this one figured out; you can stay in your cage.* Three magic words should therefore come more easily to us and to our shepherds than to corporate titans: "I don't know," as in, "I don't know the right strategy; I need the ideas and input of my flock."

## Our Mission: Leading Others to Faith, Freedom, and Love of Christ

Here's another advantage our church brings to strategy-setting: unlike many human institutions, we know exactly where we want to go. That's more advantageous than may at first seem. So many worldly organizations must regularly rethink the "ends" they're aiming for, their earthly mission. What should the bookstore chain become when Amazon comes along, the film manufacturer when digital cameras are invented, or the video rental outlets once streaming video takes hold?

For us as a church? We don't have to rethink our "ends": we know what we want to achieve, always have known and always will. As Vatican II put it, our church's mission is to "lead others to the faith, freedom, and love of Christ." That mission will not change. We might say it in different ways: to make Jesus's name, "known and loved," for example, or to help create God's Kingdom, or, in Jesus's own words, to "go and make disciples of all nations." But, essentially, we know our unchanging mission, the "ends" we seek, to use strategy-speak. That's a huge advantage relative to so many human enterprises.

So, too, are the resources we bring to mission, our "means," in strategy-speak. Sure, most parishes feel resource-constrained. But good strategies enable institutions to "flip the script" by focusing not on deprivation but on leveraging their abundant resources. We're a global church, active in some 200 countries; we comprise more than 200,000 parishes and thousands of schools, hospitals, and social service centers. Above all, a billion talented adherents are gifted with every expertise any organization could ever want. Surely we can craft a winning strategy from such riches.

Provided that, like those soldiers in the Alps, we get going and take the risks inherent in striking out in new directions. Ironically, our advantages can also become a liability. We may not feel the same urgency for change as less-abundantly resourced organizations feel. They know they will wither and die if they cannot catapult themselves onto a more promising trajectory; in contrast, our church can weather decades of stagnation and still find some evidence to convince ourselves that things are okay: every year, for example, we read that the world's population of baptized Catholics has increased. Accordingly, we drift into satisfied complacency because we don't dig deep enough to reveal the worrying facts beneath that superficial good news.

Consider, for example, the 2012 global synod convened by Pope Benedict XVI to discuss the so-called New Evangelization, which, to oversimplify, refers to the ways in which Catholicism can deepen the faith of current members and present its message to nonmembers. Few topics could be more crucial at this moment when church participation has been steadily eroding.

The synod's preparatory document left no doubt that change was imperative, proclaiming, "The Urgency of a New Evangelization." The document all but screamed for new strategies, peppered with phrases like, "the situation is requiring the Church to consider, in an entirely new way, how she proclaims and transmits the faith." The document rejected, "a *status quo* mentality. . . . Today, a "business as usual" attitude can no longer be the case."

I was thrilled. A logjam is breaking, I thought. New ways of attacking our challenges will be forthcoming. But the final document lacked urgency and new ideas, arguing that, "We need not invent new strategies." I was stunned to read it. Tens of millions of Catholics have grown lukewarm or abandoned Catholicism entirely in recent decades, yet no new strategies are needed? With all respect, new strategies are exactly what we need. Granted, the synod was making a broader point: "We need not invent new strategies," their document said, "as if the gospel were a product to be placed in the market of religions."

Well, yes and no. To be sure, the church does not exist to profit by selling Jesus like a detergent brand; the gospel is not a product in that respect. But it's precisely because our mission is so profound that the church does need new strategies. Think of it this way: if shampoo sellers are motivated to engage consumers imaginatively, how much more dynamic and creative should we be, who believe our "product" to be life-changing, indeed life-saving? And, whether we like it or not, we *are* competing in the secular, individualistic, consumerist twenty-first-century marketplace of religions and ideas.

The church is divinely inspired and guided, but it is also a vast, complex enterprise with goals to achieve, and it won't achieve those goals without a sound plan. By saying that no new strategies are needed, these synod leaders were implicitly proclaiming that the strategy we've got now is working just fine. And that way of thinking has consequences, all of them bad. For one thing, a much-needed sense of urgency becomes lost. Four consecutive Popes have now called it "urgent" that we figure out how to present our faith in the modern world, yet how often, for example, have you heard such a call in your parish?

Or Pope John Paul II once resolved to "commit all of the church's energies" to evangelization. Do you see much on-the-ground evidence of that total commitment in your parish or diocese? Can you imagine a company that resolved to commit "all its energies" to an "urgent" goal, yet virtually no one in the organization knew about it? Frankly put, too many of our vaunted initiatives end up as little more than slogans because of the church's inability to think and act strategically.

## NAMING THE PRIORITIES THAT CAN MAKE A DIFFERENCE

Take another example. Pope Francis seemed to commit his Papacy to reversing the church's sliding fortunes, yet some of his top lieutenants seemed unsure about his priorities. The late Francis Cardinal George, then Chicago's archbishop, was surely better plugged in than you or I, yet he once told the *New York Times*: "[The Pope] says wonderful things, but he doesn't put them together all the time, so you're left at times puzzling over what his intention is. What he says is clear enough, but what does he want us to do?"

Wow. If a top Cardinal suffered such lack of clarity, imagine the priests who worked for him, much less those sitting in the pews of Chicago's parishes. Confusion or disagreement at the top is only amplified as one cascades through the organization.

Part of the problem is that Popes (or bishops, or pastors) must say and write lots of things, on lots of topics. These documents may be wonderful, but they aren't a strategy. Put differently, the church regularly breaks what I call the "three things" rule. I coined that term after an episode when a company leader had asked me to draft talking points for an address to investment banking managers. When I presented a draft to my boss, he scanned it for a minute, then said in a matter-of-fact way, "There's lots of good points here. But what are the three things?"

"Excuse me?"

"What are the three key things I will tell them to focus on?"

I won't soon forget that lesson about human nature, managerial courage, and the essence of leadership. That boss was convinced that teams can sustain focus on only a few priorities. By ticking through a laundry list of priorities and analysis, I would ensure only that the group remembered nothing in particular, or would cherry-pick the ideas that resonated with their personal preferences.

Admittedly, it's incredibly difficult for an organizational leader to identify the "three things" (or four, or five, as the case may be). Every large organization faces myriad challenges. But great leaders manifest the judgment to discern key priorities and the courage to plant a stake in the ground by publicly proclaiming them. They lift our horizons: we see our individual roles as connected to the bigger cause. We understand ourselves as one team and no longer feel inclined to indulge in internal spitball fights (say, between liberal and conservative Catholics), because we know that we must coalesce around these few vital goals for our beloved church to thrive. We don't feel like bystanders who are watching the bosses, because now we know priorities and are empowered to contribute.

## LET'S START SINGING FROM THE SAME STRATEGIC HYMNBOOK

By standing in front of J. P. Morgan's seventy top leaders across Europe and saying, "these three things are really, really important," that boss unleashed great power that we are not yet tapping as a church. And the message was amplified when those managers subsequently repeated those priorities to their own subordinates, and subordinates quickly discovered that everyone was stressing the same things, singing from the same hymnbook, so to speak.

When we Catholics attend Mass, we sing from the same hymnbook. On pronouncements of faith and dogma, we Catholics absolutely sing from the same hymnbook (or else we get an unwelcome phone call from the Vatican Congregation for the Doctrine of the Faith). But when it comes to revitalizing our church, we don't even have a hymnbook.

We can't articulate the three things (or five, as the case will be). What priorities are most crucial right now as we steward the church into the twenty-first century? I asked that question of various Catholics and heard a very wide range of answers, too wide. Many have no idea what the church's priorities are or should be; others offered their own ideas, typically focused on a particular church doctrine or practice that irritated them. Taken together, the ideas were a cacophonous collection of notes that didn't coalesce into the integrated harmony of a coherent approach.

We will never succeed like that. An empowered army can create a supremely chaotic mess if their energies are not channeled. Think of a billion Catholics, like so many loose cannons, each firing in whatever direction looks promising, with more than a few of us firing at each other, as is unfortunately the case now.

The solution is not micromanagement; rather, we need to articulate strategic priorities in a way that will empower individual Catholics, parishes, and ministries to take initiative. Strategy is not a spectator sport that leaves one billion team members on the sidelines, watching a relative handful in Rome. Vatican and Papal initiatives are crucial, of course, but as our early Christian ancestors teach us, the action is not in headquarters but out in the field. Local leaders will know best what works in their own backyards. To put it in terms of Catholic social teaching, strategic "subsidiarity" will empower those on the scene to take all the initiative and responsibility that they legitimately can. We have loads of great parish pastors, for example, who are blessed with eager lay collaborators; we want to liberate their energies and creativity on the Lord's behalf.

That's why the following chapters will not delve into specific prescriptions, like what kind of devotions or prayer groups to launch in Manila's or Manhattan's parishes. Micromanagement is never smart strategy, above all when the micromanager lacks the expertise of those on the ground. I myself, for example, wouldn't have a clue what outreach program will draw young adults in Omaha or Harare, but I bet there are talented young adult ministers who do: let's frame a strategy to maximize their chance to lead the church forward in all the ways they can.

That doesn't mean we want ministries to labor in splendid isolation. We want every person, parish, and ministry to feel solidarity with the rest of the church and an impulse to collaborate. Energy and excellence will be unleashed when, for example, American and Kenyan Catholic hospitals actively share best practices; or when Detroit's parishes, hospitals, and social service agencies all sit down to explore how they might witness together and leverage each other's efforts. We Catholics enjoy the world's most impressive global network, but in many respects, that's only on paper. We will lift our ministries out of their specialized silos, so that we can realize our full promise as a network.

Above all, we want a strategy that embodies the church's core mission, not anyone's personal agenda. We're not inventing a different mission for the church but expressing our timeless mission in language that enables every person, parish, and ministry to contribute more proactively. Accordingly, what follows is nothing more (or less) than a reflection of Jesus's core commands: "to make disciples of all nations" and to "love God with all your heart . . . [and] love your neighbor as yourself" (Matt. 22: 37–39). Or those with a predilection for sophisticated theological terminology could map the strategy against what Pope Benedict XVI called, "the Church's threefold responsibility: proclaiming the word of God (kerygma-martyria), celebrating the sacraments (leitourgia), and exercising the ministry of charity (diakonia)"; these three lofty ideas are broadened and translated into more accessible language.

The EASTeR project is a pathway to accomplishing all of this. We will focus on becoming a more *Entrepreneurial* and *Accountable* church that *Serves* all in need, *Transforms* the spiritual lives of its members, and *Reaches out* widely to engage the world around us. Entrepreneurial and Accountable; Serve, Transform, and Reach out: those five ideas can revitalize our church, if embraced both bottom-up and top-down, that is, by individual believers and by those with hierarchical authority. It's an EASTeR strategy for an Easter people, who are filled with hope, joy, and renewed energy. Thus, the five pillars of our EASTeR project for church renewal.

## BE ENTREPRENEURIAL

I was born into a world where everyone used the same brand of telephone and where young people dutifully embraced their parents' religion.

That world is gone, and only the entrepreneurially minded will thrive in the world that has replaced it, where individuals increasingly choose where they worship, honor their church's beliefs only selectively, leave churches that don't address their needs, are highly skeptical of organized religion, or are so entranced by modernity's material charms that a commitment to a spiritual path seems stifling and antiquated. Indeed, even among committed Catholics, our church must figure out how to adapt to an individualistic, diverse modern world where some crave exuberant Pentecostal-style worship and others a hushed Latin Mass.

This is the world to which the Holy Spirit calls us to minister, and we will only succeed by becoming more Spirit-led, like those early Christian leaders who adapted their rituals, language, worship styles, and organizational structure in order to engage the new cultures they encountered. Spirit-led entrepreneurs behave differently because they see opportunities where others see only problems: they see a Church abundantly blessed with gifted men and women and will imagine ways to unlock all that talent, just as that Nairobi pastor developed new roles in which Lucy, Samuel, and the other jumuiya leaders could serve the church.

The word "entrepreneurial" will trigger alarm bells among some: does it imply a freelance church where religious hucksters can twist dogma to suit their ambitions and make themselves rich? I'm saying no such thing; no idea advanced in this book contravenes church teaching. But I am saying this: our mission is to lead others to an encounter with Jesus that changes them and the world, and we are not accomplishing that mission nearly as well as we can and will. To improve, we will become more nimble, exploit modern technology, express our message creatively, share information more widely, empower our laity, vary prayer and worship styles to accommodate our very diverse populations, offer meaningful spiritual growth opportunities, make better use of our talent, and, overall, be not only open to new ways of doing things but eagerly seek new approaches. Doing all that will require an entrepreneurial spirit.

## BE ACCOUNTABLE

How do we know when we are successful in our parishes and other ministries? Accountable organizations can answer that question.

To cite one example of many: my Catechism teaches, "those who are oppressed by poverty are the object of a preferential love" on the church's part. *Preferential* love implies a clear commitment: how do we verify that we are living that commitment in deeds? Sure, we could point to examples, like church-run soup kitchens or a hundred other worthy efforts. But tossing off anecdotal examples is not the same as holding oneself accountable: the plural of anecdote is not data. We will therefore be more conscientious in monitoring, evaluating, and assessing how well we are fulfilling the various mandates Jesus gave us, whether our stewardship of money, our service to poor communities, or the effectiveness of our parishes in drawing members closer to the Lord.

The process of becoming a more accountable church will be uncomfortable; it will require us to ask ourselves difficult questions. We believe, for example, that the church facilitates spiritual growth through a deeper encounter with Jesus, but we don't really know how consistently that is happening; we don't ask ourselves or parishioners whether that's going well or poorly, much less track our results over time. The process of doing so will not come naturally to us, but what we learn will make us a more effective, credible church.

## SERVE THE POOR AND MARGINALIZED

Amidst rampant individualism and consumerism, our twenty-first-century church will differentiate itself by a countercultural commitment: we will serve and seek justice for all who are poor, marginalized, or excluded. This will become core to our "brand," so to speak, in every parish, hospital, and ministry.

Ultimately, of course, this priority has nothing to do with branding and everything to do with Jesus's teaching that our neighbors are all those in need. And it is by loving and serving those in need, Jesus told us, that we demonstrate our love for the Lord. Pope John Paul II once spoke of, "the fascinating power of love," and we will fascinate an increasingly self-absorbed world by our commitment to selfless love.

## TRANSFORM EACH WORSHIPPER'S HEART AND SOUL

Our church's mission, says Vatican II, is to lead others, "to the faith, freedom, and love of Christ." Those words make clear that our church should be a place where lives are transformed for the good, where "conversion" happens, not primarily in the sense of changing from one religious belief to another, but in line with the word's Latin roots, which connote a turning around, or a return. If folks are on the wrong path in life, we will inspire them to "turn around" and walk in the way of the Lord. If they are already growing in faith, we will enable a turn toward even greater peace, faith, and inner joy.

We're not currently fulfilling this part of our mission well enough. Consider, for example, that a whopping 71 percent of former Catholics in the United States who now worship elsewhere say that they left us in part because their spiritual needs were not being met. The Holy Spirit is surely speaking to us through that damning statistic. Let's commit to transforming our church into one where transformation happens.

## REACH OUT TO THE WORLD BEYOND OUR CHURCH DOORS

A Catholic Church long accustomed to "cradle to grave" Catholics who "pay, pray, and obey" must now engineer a massive culture shift to thrive in a world where increasing numbers of people find the church irrelevant and never come knocking on our doors. As Pope Francis memorably put it, "A Church that does not go out of itself, sooner or later, sickens from the stale air of closed rooms."

A more outgoing Church begins, for example, with something as simple as letting others know that you welcome them. Consider this: nearly 87 percent of Evangelical Christians invited someone to participate in their church's activities during the last twelve months. What is the equivalent statistic for Catholics? We don't even know. I can report only my own experience: I have never been urged from a pulpit to invite someone to Mass or to participate alongside us in one of our charitable ministries; I've almost never been personally welcomed while attending Mass away from home. We will change all that and foster a wide-ranging culture of engagement.

## FIVE PRINCIPLES, BUT ONE CALLING

Don't think of these five ideas as a laundry list of discrete priorities that have little to do with each other. Exactly the opposite: each leverages the others, a fancy way of saying that when we execute one priority well, the other priorities will all benefit. In following chapters, for example, we will meet Christians whose spiritual lives were transformed by their experience of serving the sick, or who reached out to engage the world by serving the marginalized. Looked at one way, serving, transforming, and reaching out are three distinct activities, yet ultimately they are three dimensions of our one calling as Christians.

Already, we Catholics profess the same Lord Jesus and the same Eucharist. Now we will also enjoy the consolation of aligning our actions more closely. We will learn from fellow Catholics who are pursuing those same goals, whether in the next parish or across the world. We will share the good ideas we've hatched and benchmark ourselves against neighboring parishes who may be doing things better, deeply committed to holding ourselves accountable and always improving what we do on the Lord's behalf. Our solidarity will deepen as we celebrate our fellow Catholics' successes and feel their struggles as our own.

## HAVING FUN AND SPREADING JOY AS WE REBUILD

One final point before elaborating these five pillars in following chapters. Not only will commitment to them engender a flourishing Church, but the journey itself will be energizing and fun. There has been too little of that. Ordinary churchgoers may have felt themselves discouraged bystanders over recent decades, seeing parishes and grammar schools close, wondering about the ever-dwindling supply of priests, or watching "progressive" and "traditional" thought leaders engage in an embarrassing, church-sabotaging blame game.

Enough of all that. Pope Francis called for a more joyful church, and this strategy invites talented Christians to wield their gifts joyfully and to have some fun along the way. Like all good strategies, this one can be supercharged by "top-down" leadership as bishops and others in authority embrace and disseminate it. But our strategy doesn't depend solely on top-down leadership; no one gatekeeper will derail the movement to renew our church. Rather, every Catholic and every Catholic ministry can discuss these ideas and conceive of ways to implement them, without waiting for instructions from "headquarters."

Let the Spirit blow where it wills, and let leadership blossom accordingly. The following chapters help us to get started.

## *Pray, Reflect, Discuss, and Act*

- What's your initial reaction to the EASTeR project's five pillars? What seems most relevant for your parish or ministry (and for the global church) right now? What seems to be missing?

- Evaluate your parish (or ministry or diocese) against the five pillars: in which of the five areas is your parish/ministry strongest (and why)? Where weakest?

- As you contemplate the EASTeR project: what strikes you as "easy wins"? That is, what could you, your parish, or your ministry begin doing tomorrow that would show immediate impact in one or more of the five priority areas?

- How, concretely, could your parish or ministry begin thinking and acting more strategically? How could you develop and disseminate a more holistic strategy (whether this book's or your own) among congregants, staff, and other stakeholders?

# CHAPTER SIX

# The Catholic Elephant Can Dance

## *An Entrepreneurial Church*

"I'VE NEVER SEEN SO MANY ENERGIZED YOUNG PEOPLE IN A CHURCH before," says one amazed guy to Fr. Emmanuel. A few minutes earlier, before things got started, the same guy's worried take had been: "How's it gonna work? I don't understand how it's gonna work." Fr. Emmanuel had told him just to step back and let the Holy Spirit take over.

"It" refers to the Catholic Hackathon that Fr. Emmanuel Taylor had spearheaded at St. Dominic's, a San Francisco parish served by Emmanuel's Dominican congregation. What's a hackathon? Truth be told, Fr. Emmanuel didn't know either, at first. Granted, he's technically inclined: he was a scientist at the Woods Hole Oceanographic Institution before discovering his priestly vocation (cue the lame jokes: he left oceanography to become a fisher of men). But oceanography didn't equip him to code software, much less organize hackathons.

St. Dominic's is one of those urban parishes that become magnets for young adults who migrate to big cities for work. And, this being San Francisco, "young adult" often means "Silicon Valley techie." You couldn't swing a cat (or a thurible) around that church without hitting a computer geek. Emmanuel was haunted by all that talent. He wanted to unleash it on the church's behalf but didn't know how. No worry, his tech-savvy parishioners knew. One of them told him, "What we do in technology are hackathons. You just present a problem, provide food, and people will come."

## What Digital Pentecost Looks Like

Could it be that easy? Emmanuel was unsure but game. He barely advertised his hackathon, yet sixty Catholic techies showed up, all keen to develop apps or other web-enabled tools that could help communicate the faith. Then Emmanuel basically got out of the way, "It was amazing. At the outset, attendees with project ideas briefly pitched their proposals to the whole group." Then, the techies organized themselves into work groups by gravitating toward whichever idea had intrigued them. Then, says Emmanuel, "within a half hour, everyone is buzzing, everyone is working. It just happens so easily here because people know what to do."

By the next afternoon, a lot of Chinese food had been devoured, and rough prototypes of a handful of apps had emerged. Like "Preach Back": imagine a smart phone app that enables a post-Mass dialogue with the priest and among congregants about the ideas shared in the homily, a tech-facilitated way to keep God's word alive in the community. Or, when the collection basket was passed around, imagine if, instead of digging out your wallet, you could yank out your cell phone and make your offering by tapping the Hackathon's collection basket app. (News flash for us fifty-something troglodytes who still organize the offertory collection the Stone Age way: lots of young adults don't bother with wallets or purses. The digital wallet is racing ahead, and our church is falling behind.) And for the times when we Catholics are not in church but absorbed in our chaotically busy work lives? Well, there's a Hackathon app for that too: "Bible moments" would prompt us periodically with a scripture verse or short reflection, injecting a spiritual mini-break into our work lives.

One of the Dominicans at the Hackathon said it felt like a "Digital Pentecost," as if the Holy Spirit had inspired tongues of digital fire over techie apostles. Well, our challenged church surely needs a new Pentecost, which is why an earlier chapter exhorted us to call God's Holy Spirit into our midst. But we and those in authority have to do more than just call on the Holy Spirit; we also need to use wit and imagination, so that we are well positioned when the Holy Spirit's showers of inspiration wash over us.

That's just what Fr. Emmanuel did. So many talented believers were sitting in his congregation each Sunday. Their souls were being nourished, but they were like that gospel talent that is buried in the ground by the fearful servant. No one had thought of investing that talent by tapping their unique skills to help lead the church forward. Fr. Emmanuel and his hackers were answering Pope John Paul II's call to share our good news in a way that would be, "new in its ardor, new in its methods, and new in its expression." Way back in 1983, John Paul II could see that much of Europe, and a majority of young adults, were beginning to regard Catholicism with a big yawn, if not with outright hostility. Interest in the church was fading in countries that had long been considered its very heart, like France, Spain, Ireland, or Brazil.

And so, the Pope pleaded, we need new methods, expressions, and ardor. This chapter's theme is new methods and expressions, or, as we put it, an entrepreneurial spirit. Without that? Well, join me in a thought experiment that makes a point. Jot down the really significant, impactful new methods and approaches that have debuted in your parish, or the church at large, since the Pope made that plea more than three decades ago.

My list was almost empty. I guess we could count the Pope's Twitter account, though any objective observer would consider the church quite late and lagging in social media and in using technology generally. Some readers may have thought of World Youth Day or the EWTN television network: sorry, both more than three decades old.

Enough said. Let's end the drought and become a more innovative church. I know that the word "entrepreneurial" is a tongue twister, and the word's connotation may rub some readers the wrong way. Aren't entrepreneurs those businesspeople whose sole pursuit is fame and fortune? We typically associate entrepreneurs with start-up businesses, not with a tradition-rich church. But for that treasured tradition to thrive, we will have to start channeling the entrepreneurial spirit of our first-century ancestors, who preserved our tradition's heart precisely through innovation.

So how will we go about it? After studying another case study of Catholic entrepreneurship, we'll learn from experts in the field and reflect on four questions: How do we develop new ideas? How do we then circulate them around our global church network? How do we fund new ideas and support those "Holy Entrepreneurs" who are courageous enough to propose new approaches? How do we even know that an idea is good?

The word entrepreneur may conjure up Mark Zuckerberg, Facebook's founder, who engineered a world-changing idea that made him a multibillionaire. But world-changing ideas are not this chapter's focus. For sure, we should always hope and pray for these. Mother Teresa's Missionaries of Charity have grown to some 4,500 sisters and are a global icon of what "love thy neighbor" looks like. Likewise, with the Jesuit Refugee Service, which has grown from a standing start to now serve nearly a million people in fifty countries. Or take EWTN, the mass media network that was founded in a garage and now broadcasts globally. Those have all been entrepreneurial "home runs" for the church, great ideas that started with nothing and succeeded beyond anyone's imagination. But this chapter focuses less on "home runs" than on "singles," the more modest initiatives that you or I might launch tomorrow.

Nor is this chapter primarily about media, technology, young adults, or further incarnations of Fr. Emmanuel's hackathon, vital though all those will be to a church that hopes to thrive in the twenty-first century. Rather, this chapter's call is for all of us, whether young adult or geezer, whether launching a brand-new ministry or administering a century-old parish. Entrepreneurial spirit is not only manifested in lines of computer code but in comments like: *here's an effort that's not really succeeding in our parish, and I'd like a shot at doing it differently*; or *we've never thought of doing something like this before; let's try*; or from a pastor, bishop, or ministry leader: *yes, let's try; you take the lead; if we fail, it will be worthwhile anyway: we'll learn so much along the way.*

Recall one of this book's mantras: everyone leads. We will only accomplish our mission in this rapidly changing world if a critical mass of us embrace the leadership call that comes with baptism, and one of its expressions is entrepreneurial spirit. Few of us may have the technology skills of Fr. Emmanuel's hackers, but almost any one of us, for example, could have done what Katharina Maloney (nee Fassler) and colleagues did.

## Why Didn't You or I Think of That?

Katharina is German, and a member of the Emmanuel Community, a movement in some sixty countries that helps Catholics pursue holiness. In fact, movements like Emmanuel, the Community of St. Egidio, Focolare, and about a hundred others are under-heralded examples of Holy Entrepreneurship and spawning grounds for entrepreneurs. Many Americans are unfamiliar with these innovative associations, often founded in just the last few decades to build community among groups of Catholics while helping them to lead committed faith lives during this era when many parishes lack vibrancy and practicing Catholics can feel like lone oddballs amidst the secular culture.

Anyway, Katharina and a few friends, inspired by devotional practices that had touched their own lives, conceived "Nightfever," which they launched in a Bonn (Germany) church in 2005. The basic idea is so simple that you slap your head and wonder why we didn't think of it two decades ago. The recipe? Identify a well-trafficked church in your city, the kind of church that hundreds of pedestrians pass by and barely notice as they walk to restaurants or from their workplace to the train station.

Then turn that church into a festival of light: illuminate the church interior and the entrance steps with hundreds of candles, throw open the doors, provide choral or recorded music inside, expose the Eucharist for adoration, and station volunteers outside to invite passersby for a short visit: to pray or simply to unwind in the peaceful interior, ponder a scripture passage, jot down a prayer intention that has weighed on their heart, consult a priest after twenty years away from church, or even just to satisfy their curiosity about a place they've never entered before. That simple.

What's not to love about the idea? It's fresh and creative, unlike anything the church had been doing. It's not costly or time consuming, and it doesn't require specialized skills to undertake. It appeals to devout Christians yet also appeals to mere curiosity seekers as a nonthreatening window into Christian spirituality. And it's eminently transferable: you can plop it down in New York or Montevideo, and it will work equally well. And it has worked well: more than 2,000 Nightfevers have been mounted in nearly 400 locations and some dozen countries.

Any one of us could have conceived and launched something like it with a few friends. So why don't we have lots more examples of similarly fresh initiatives? Not just new methods for evangelizing or reaching out, like Nightfever, but new approaches to administering parishes, running retreats, raising money, interacting with young adults, training catechists, doing Bible study, leveraging social media, you name it. Why don't we have countless more Katharinas? How will we foster a culture of Holy Entrepreneurship in our church? Let's examine her story and that of Fr. Emmanuel, through an entrepreneurial lens, by asking four questions that will pinpoint shortcomings and opportunities for us to bend our culture in a more innovative direction.

## Empower More Bottom-Up Leadership

*How will we develop new ideas?* Katharina and Fr. Emmanuel exemplify two vital ingredients of tomorrow's more entrepreneurial church culture: bottom-up leadership and positive deviancy. Bottom-up leadership—no higher-up in the Vatican or diocesan "headquarters" commissioned Night-fever or the Hackathon. Katharina and Emmanuel conceived those ideas and ran with them. In fact, Katharina thought carefully before pitching the first Nightfever to a parish. She wanted a parish that might agree quickly; she didn't want to have the idea bog down in endless church bureaucracy and watch momentum drain away as her enthused co-entrepreneurs slowly became discouraged. She had seen that happen while trying previous initiatives on the church's behalf: "I notice there is a lot of fear to walk on new paths. Fear of criticism from higher ups, fear of putting off a few people in the parish, even just with straightforward things like a new time for Mass. The emphasis seems mostly on preserving things."

That's not the mindset of "positive deviants" like Katharina. The fancy term may sound perverted, but it's a well-established behavioral theory. Namely: just because someone has the most information and best resources, that doesn't mean they will generate the solutions. Instead, winning ideas often surface from relative outsiders, whether Mark Zuckerberg or Katharina, whose advantage is not power or information but simply the will and imagination to solve problems. The lesson? Organizations often respond to emerging challenges in exactly the wrong way: they turn to the well-informed, long-experienced insider-manager for solutions. But those folks often come up with more of the same kind of thinking that got the organization into trouble in the first place. If you need a breakthrough approach to a vexing challenge, don't go to the headquarters bureaucrat: find the positive deviant out in the field.

So many of the church's new models and innovations have come bottom-up from our positive deviants rather than top-down from the Vatican or elsewhere: think of Francis of Assisi, Mother Seton, or so many other religious order founders; in our own era, what about Fe y Alegria's Fr. Vélaz, EWTN's Mother Angelica, and countless other holy entrepreneurs from outside the system.

In fact, Mother Angelica, that endearingly cantankerous, lone ranger nun who started a global Catholic media empire from a garage, perfectly illumines the point. Upon her death, Archbishop Charles Chaput praised her imaginative spunk by indirectly critiquing his fellow bishops' lack thereof: "Mother Angelica succeeded at a task the nation's bishops themselves couldn't achieve. She founded and grew a network that appealed to everyday Catholics."

Well, I might see it differently than Archbishop Chaput. I wouldn't expect him and his bishop colleagues to be the church's innovators. Take my experience by analogy. I myself rose through corporate ranks to become a cog in the managerial machine, which was the last place where new ideas would surface: we inhabited an echo chamber of like-minded managerial peers who all went to the same schools, thought the same way, worried about keeping control, were afraid of making mistakes, didn't want to upset the big bosses, and, therefore, never rocked the boat.

But since Archbishop Chaput opened the door on this topic, I'll step through it. Based on my own managerial experiences, my question for those in church hierarchy would never be: *why aren't you yourselves coming up with more innovations in our troubled times?* Rather, I would ask: *what can you do to find and nurture many more "Holy Entrepreneurs"?* We must have many out there, yet they seem to be like hidden talents. We have too little innovation to show for ourselves, compared to some highly agile non-Catholic churches that have exploded in recent decades, often thanks to creative new worship approaches, fresh music ministries, groundbreaking use of communications and social media, or other initiatives.

## END THE TYRANNY OF GROUPTHINK

That's why smart organizations often set up oases of creativity, "idea labs" where innovators get to tinker with ideas, away from the stultifying, imagination-sapping dynamics of headquarters. GE, for example, prizes "FastWorks," where senior executives hear pitches for new programs or products and award, on the spot, enough seed funding to test the most promising ideas in a ninety-day implementation "sprint."

Well, we as a church ought to embrace such approaches even more fervently than corporations do, simply because we're even more prone to the dangers of groupthink than they are. So many of our hierarchical leaders around the world have studied the same things at the same few schools in the same city of Rome, a great spiritual and theological formation, for sure, but the creative instinct can be dampened when too many organizational leaders are formed in the same mold.

## Become More Shameless

*Once we generate a good idea, how will we spread it?* How did that first Nightfever, for example, lead to 2,000 more of them? Some of Katharina's fellow entrepreneurs were university students who, apostle-like, enthusiastically spread the concept when they relocated to study abroad. Eventually, the Diocese of Cologne brought the idea in house, turning the original entrepreneurs' concept into a formalized church initiative, led by a priest; that institutional church status theoretically gave it a platform to grow even further.

Theoretically. The glass-full perspective? The idea has already spread to multiple cities. The glass-half-empty perspective? Some of the founding lay entrepreneurs felt a bit marginalized as the project management became, well, "clericalized." Priestly collaboration is wonderful, but in this case the founders weren't drawn in as collaborators but felt cut off. And, while the institutional church network would theoretically offer a neural network around which great ideas can rocket quickly, our global church network is typically more sclerotic than vibrant. Granted, a Papal pronouncement on dogma will rocket around the global church in a day. But promising new administrative, fundraising, or ministry ideas may languish indefinitely.

Nightfever, for instance, came to New York not because it coursed through institutional church channels but because a lay "holy entrepreneur" read about it in a magazine and resolved to launch it in New York.

Thank God for the serendipity that an imaginative New York Catholic just happened to pick up that magazine, but great organizations don't rely on serendipity to put great ideas into the right people's hands.

The *Harvard Business Review* article, "Change Without Pain," hailed the impulse of successful organizations to: "reward shameless borrowing." We're not shameless enough. Too many parishes and ministries labor in splendid isolation: we're not adept at propelling promising ideas around the system, at sharing one parish's good practices with sister parishes across the country, not to mention around the world.

Let's say, for example, that Fr. Emmanuel and his hackers end up perfecting a couple of apps, or that some parish originates a great new young adult outreach model. Word of such ideas should bound through our parish and diocesan networks. Alas, it doesn't yet work like that. We are falling far short of our potential as a network. But the good news is that we will easily get better. Entrepreneurial spirit and social media technologies will turn us into the robust network that we can and should be.

## Nurture Our Holy Entrepreneurs

*How will we support and nurture those who are courageous enough to propose new approaches?* After Fr. Emmanuel's hackathon attendees sketched out their skeletal apps on that Digital Pentecost, they returned to their full-time jobs on Monday, and the project stalled a bit. Fr. Emmanuel has scrounged around for money to pay developers to complete each app's detailed coding.

His predicament is a great metaphor: the guy is sitting in the heart of Silicon Valley, where waterfalls of cash gush all over promising ideas. Yet not over holy ones. We don't just need Holy Entrepreneurs, but Holy Venture Capital and Holy Angel Investors, that is, resources for funding promising new ideas. As we'll see, successful innovation only flourishes in a supportive ecosystem. We're making it too hard for intrepid entrepreneurs like Fr. Emmanuel and Katharina, Fr. Chris Walsh the Philly pastor, and so many others. All were self-starters. No one trained them; no one mentored them. Nor, frankly, did they get lots of pats on the back when their good ideas got traction. There's a better way to do all this, as we'll learn shortly.

But first, it's worth reminding ourselves just why we all need to start thinking more like entrepreneurs, and why that doesn't come naturally in any large institution.

## Use "Jesus Logic" to Nurture Great Initiatives

*How will we know if an idea is good?* Is Nightfever a good idea? The Preach Back app? Looked at one way, vastly so: hundreds of people have attended Nightfever in dozens of locations, and the initiative is still growing. Many people, Katharina told me, "go to confession for the first time in a long time, or discover the church as a place of silence and inspiration and resolve to start going to church more often again."

But who knows how many attendees really return to church after Nightfever? And, anyway, countless churches welcome more people each Sunday at Mass than will attend a Nightfever. Nor does Nightfever generate donations.

By worldly business logic, there are better ways to spend time than Nightfever: we could generate a more certain return by improving what already happens in church each Sunday, rather than trying unproven ideas. But there is worldly logic and there is Jesus's logic, and Jesus told us to leave the ninety-nine sheep behind to seek out the one that has strayed; and Jesus left a town where his message was finding fruit because he felt called to proclaim the Good News, "to the other towns," that is, to reach out to new people on new frontiers.

Unless we can revive Jesus-logic, we will never become sufficiently entrepreneurial, because of what I call the "curse of success." It's hard enough to run hard after one straying sheep when you have ninety-nine others to tend. But we have far more than ninety-nine: there are 1.2 billion of us Catholics, and thousands of schools, hospitals, and parishes to tend. It's hardly worth the effort to introduce ourselves to one new person with such a vast institution to maintain. Our apostolic ancestors, in contrast, counted virtually no sheep and eagerly pursued every opportunity to grow their flock; we may have lost that knack.

That's the curse of success. You become a vast, sprawling institution and forget the spunky spirit that catalyzed your success in the first place. Think of iconic companies like Microsoft or Apple, both launched in garages by founders who embodied the entrepreneurial spirit that we need to recover. Both Bill Gates and Steve Jobs, for example, never settled for the *status quo*, restlessly pursued new ways to do things, risked failure, and persevered through setbacks. They shunned the "we've always done it this way" mindset and cultivated a "must be a better way" mindset. They inspired others to dream and labor alongside them.

That's just like our great church builders of generations past. Apostles like Paul founded Christian communities where none had existed and conceived novel conceptual approaches that intrigued pagan, philosophy-loving Greek thinkers. Or take religious orders like the Franciscans, Dominicans, Jesuits, or Daughters of Charity, all founded by visionaries who lacked organizational status and capital. These founders embodied "positive defiance" at its best. Resource poor but imagination rich, they envisioned completely new models of religious life, and their fresh thinking attracted scores of recruits to embark on a pioneering adventure.

I earlier mentioned my board service at Catholic Health Initiatives (CHI), the large Catholic hospital system that counts more than 100 hospitals. But our foundresses counted only on their ingenuity, like the Sisters of St. Francis of Philadelphia, two of whom were once missioned to Lancaster County, Pennsylvania. Their resources? Exactly $2.86 and two apples. Their results? Among many other ministerial feats, they founded the county's first hospital (its successor system still operates). How the heck did two sisters turn two dollars and two apples into a hospital? Surely the Holy Spirit had something to do with it, but so did their can-do spirit.

Which now gets us to the problem that comes with success and scale. See, CHI today faces the same kind of challenge that confronts Microsoft and our global church: hanging on to that adventurous spirit that first animated us. That's harder to do after you've grown from two apples to lots of hospital buildings (or parishes, schools, and chanceries, as the case may be). The mindset of new recruits changes: they no longer join with the expectation of heading onto frontiers to launch something new. Rather, they expect to run and maintain well-established parishes. That expectation alone can influence who is attracted to join, their attitudes, and their training. As hierarchies proliferate to manage the large infrastructure, careerism and bureaucratic thinking infect the organization. A few bright recruits might eventually start to dream about climbing the ladder and becoming bishops, not about bootstrapping start-ups like Nightfever.

In the early days, a church or a Microsoft willingly takes prudent risks: there is everything to gain and very little to lose. Then, decades and lots of successes later, risk-averse bureaucrats become too obsessed with preserving what already exists. With our church's massive scale, it can become incredibly difficult to maintain the entrepreneurial spirit of Paul the Apostle, of those sisters with their two apples, of Francis of Assisi, or of all others who have renewed our church over the centuries.

## Make the Church Elephant Dance Again

I'm reminded again of Lou Gerstner, the legendary leader who is lionized as IBM's savior (pardon the word). We earlier quoted his maxim that "No institution will go through fundamental change unless it believes it is in deep trouble." And once the institution acknowledges the imperative to change? Then, the title of Gerstner's book becomes relevant: *Who Says Elephants Can't Dance?*

Though that imagery may offend, our church has its elephantine qualities: we're large, with such well-established ways of doing things that disseminating new approaches can feel as daunting as making that elephant dance. But we must now dance again if we are to reverse the awful trends highlighted earlier. We can surely do it; let's just reclaim the spirit of sainted entrepreneurs who built or renewed the church. We honor them in stained glass windows; we will now honor them by imitating their spirit.

So how will we get started? I scratched my head over that question before the path forward suddenly appeared before my eyes. Not as a heavenly apparition (I'm not that holy), but literally: I saw part of our answer scribbled on a whiteboard one afternoon while presenting on leadership at Acumen, an organization that identifies and nurtures "social entrepreneurs," that is, individuals committed to finding cutting-edge approaches to tackling environmental or poverty-related challenges.

During a break in my presentation, I noticed a whiteboard, scrawled with some of Acumen's guiding principles: "We catalyze entrepreneurs to solve the problems of poverty. . . . We develop leaders with the determination and moral imagination to. . . . We share ideas that accelerate solutions to poverty. . . . We build platforms that drive change."

Catalyze entrepreneurs; develop leaders; accelerate solutions; drive change. We don't see those phrases enough in our church. To be sure, we're a church, not a nongovernmental organization like Acumen. But our priorities should be animated by that same energetic drive. For example: we accelerate solutions for those who cannot find God in their lives; or we catalyze entrepreneurs who are figuring out how to attract young adults to the church; or we develop leaders with the determination and moral imagination to fight injustice.

Just as our early Christian ancestors eagerly harvested the Roman Empire's administrative insights, I started asking leading social entrepreneurs how we could better identify and nurture our own "holy entrepreneurs." I put that question to Jacqueline Novogratz, Acumen's president. And I picked Matt Bannick's brain, along with that of his colleague Sal Giambanco: they help lead the Omidyar Network, which invests in people and organizations that are committed "to advancing social good at the pace and scale the world needs today." And I looked up my friend Thane Kreiner, who runs the Miller Center for Social Entrepreneurship at Santa Clara University. If anyone knows how to find and support great entrepreneurs, I thought, these four certainly do: they have trained and funded many of the world's best.

Much of what they said encouraged me to believe that our elephant will be tap dancing in no time. Jacqueline Novogratz, for example, prizes people with "resilience and grit . . . a vision they can articulate clearly . . . and moral imagination." I was enthused: our church has plenty of all that. Matt Bannick believes that it "really starts with vision: do they have a clear idea of what issue they are trying to address," and then he added: "are they passionate about it?" He lauded the deep commitment of social entrepreneurs, because they are not in it for the money (just like our holy entrepreneurs, I thought); they are motivated by the mission (just as we are). As Matt puts it, they are more, "wedded to their ideas than the business guy who moves on if the money isn't there." If vision, commitment, resilience, and moral imagination are all we need, then we have at least a few million holy entrepreneurs in our midst.

## IN SEARCH OF RULE BREAKERS AND FRESH THINKERS

But not so fast. My wise friends started ticking off other qualities that I haven't seen very much, traits that we more often frown upon than prize. Jacqueline riffed about the great potential she finds in entrepreneurs who "have the courage not only to complain about the *status quo* but to do something about it. These are the rule breakers, the fresh thinkers and therefore the ones who often are marginalized by institutions. They do not play it safe." Rule breakers? Hmm. I can't think of many rule breakers who get real far in the church today. Thane spoke to me about "creative problem solving" and what he called, "guerilla skills—employing unconventional low cost tactics." Matt said that what often distinguishes the leaders in the field is "that focus on the new, that creation element, the reinvention instinct that these people have, the radicalness of it."

Even though my questions were focused on individual character traits, Matt swerved the conversation to the overall system in which promising individuals must function. What kinds of "emphases and biases," he asked, do people pick up in their training and workplaces, for example? A lot of the willingness to take risk or to shrink from it, he noted, "has to do with the environment in which they are selected, trained, moved along."

In the fancy lingo of Silicon Valley, a lot depends on the "ecosystem." In other words, it's not just finding individuals with the right stuff: we have such people in abundance. But the ecosystem is equally important: will the innovative thinkers be encouraged or discouraged; will financial resources be made available for their ideas; can they easily find mentors? Recall the stories about Katharina and Emmanuel and how they scrounged around for support or financing—symptomatic of our weak ecosystem.

Just imagine someone standing in front of bishops, principals, or pastors and calling for more "rule breakers" and people with "guerilla skills," who are energized by the "radicalness" of new approaches and ideas. That doesn't sound like a career-enhancing pitch. I envision a few bishops popping their miters after hearing that. A pastor could justifiably think, "Whoa. Exactly what 'rules' does this guy want us to start breaking? The Ten Commandments? The Catechism?"

But we can and must combine ardent devotion to our core beliefs *and* equal devotion to new ways of presenting those beliefs. Here's how a legendary former chairperson of IBM, Thomas Watson, once described this creative tension between tradition and change: "I firmly believe that any organization, in order to survive and achieve success, must have a sound set of beliefs on which it premises all its policies and actions. . . . And, finally, I believe that if an organization is to meet the challenges of a changing world, it must be prepared to change everything about itself except those beliefs."

Granted, it's harder for us to do that than it is for an IBM, for an obvious reason. God didn't reveal the mainframe computer to IBM; it was dreamed up by creative engineers, who are free to tinker with it or jettison it entirely. For us? We aren't free to jettison the Ten Commandments (and much else), because we believe that our core truths were in fact revealed by God. But our commitment to preserve our inviolable tradition can, if we're not careful, breed a culture that is far too resistant to change overall. So I asked my advisor-friends how we might foster a more entrepreneurial ecosystem.

Jacqueline Novogratz of Acumen talked about, "supporting social entrepreneurs with a network, a *posse,* to provide support, guidance, mentoring, friendship, to hold each other accountable and to expand networks and resources." That was a whole mouthful of eminently feasible ideas. Thousands of lay Catholics, for example, have launched enterprises in their work lives, and many of them would love to mentor those trying to innovate on the church's behalf.

And Thane Kreiner of Santa Clara's Miller Center spoke about another important way we can develop our promising talent: "the best entrepreneurial training for anyone is to work in a start-up. [That would help] young clerics in formation . . . to understand the challenges, and the pace at which entrepreneurs move and how they make decisions."

Insightful. Our seminarians are often trained in the opposite circumstances: in well-established parishes, not in ramshackle start-ups where leaders must make decisions on the fly. Our chronically understaffed, grassroots social service ministries could serve as the training ground for a resourceful new generation of church men and women.

But something else occurred to me: why don't we have our own Omidyars or Acumens, our own networks and organizations that train and fund holy entrepreneurs, in dioceses, nationally, and even internationally? Every one of our ministries of pastoral life, social service, health care, and education has talented innovators, and too often they languish without encouragement, training, or funding. We can and will do so much better. We can convene promising talent each year, teach core techniques, hear pitches of promising ministerial ideas, and provide seed money to prototype the best proposals.

## Not an Era of Change, but a Change of Era

Some readers may remain leery of this chapter's newfangled notions about entrepreneurship. Well, listen to your Holy Father! As Pope Francis told an Italian church convocation: "We are not living an era of change but a change of era." Accordingly, he continued, "Assume always the Spirit of the great explorers, that on the sea were passionate for navigation in open waters and were not frightened by borders and of storms. . . . May it be a free church and open to the challenges of the present, never in defense for fear of losing something."

He concluded with these words, "Dream of this church, believe it, innovate it with freedom."

That's all we have to do.

## *Pray, Reflect, Discuss, and Act*

- What element of your parish life (or ministry in which you are involved) needs a more "entrepreneurial" approach right now? Is there some creative idea, small or large, that should be launched right now?

- What initiatives have been tried in the last few years? What lessons could be learned from their success or failure? What small (or large) step could you take to foster a more entrepreneurial spirit in your parish or personal life as a Catholic leader?

- For dioceses (or nationally): Sponsor an annual "Holy Entrepreneurship Competition," inviting individuals, parish teams, or ministries to propose some new or innovative endeavor in ministry. Award seed money to help launch the winning ideas.

- For dioceses (or nationally): Conduct an annual "boot camp" to provide skills training and mentoring to staff, pastors, or bishops who have been nominated and selected for showing entrepreneurial promise.

- For the national (and global) church: Convene an annual "Catholicism 2.0 Conference" among bishops, diocesan administrators, and Catholic tech talent to identify and "hack" challenges and opportunities that could be addressed via social media or other technological innovation.

- For Catholic philanthropists: Create a "Holy Entrepreneurs Fund" to provide seed capital for the above-referenced entrepreneurship training, competitions, and conferences.

# CHAPTER SEVEN

# How Do You Know You're Successful?

## *An Accountable Church*

HOW DO WE KNOW THAT WE ARE SUCCEEDING IN OUR MISSION?

Responsible organizations ask and answer that question, all the time. They celebrate and quickly replicate successful initiatives; they fine-tune underperforming efforts out of a deep commitment to serve their mission well. And, as soon as disastrous missteps become apparent, they take immediate remedial action and learn lessons from failure.

That, in a nutshell, is the essence of accountability. We expect it from quality organizations, whether they are manufacturing widgets or educating high school students. Parents would be deeply dismayed if the school principal didn't even care whether children were succeeding in their math class. But merely *caring* about the job is insufficient; we expect principal and staff to manifest their care in deeds, by monitoring evidence like testing and benchmarking data to confirm whether things are going well or poorly. A commitment to the highest professional standards, therefore, is fundamental to accountability. So too is a healthy dose of transparency: we parents would expect access to some of the testing and benchmarking data, enough to understand that the school was delivering high-quality outcomes against its mission.

Like the school or widget manufacturer, our church has a mission, which we articulate in varying ways, depending on the context. We are here to make disciples of all nations, for example, to make the name of Jesus known and loved, to lead others to the faith, freedom, and love of

Christ, and to be good stewards of all the talent and treasure that has been entrusted to us by the Lord.

How's all that going for us? Are we as successful as we should be at fulfilling our mission? For the most part, we cannot answer these questions. We have no systematic way of explaining to ourselves, much less to the Lord, whether we have been good stewards.

But it's even worse than that. By way of analogy, recall that medical doctors, even before they consider the lofty ideals of their healing mission, are expected to honor a more basic human duty: *Primum non Nocere*, that is: First, do no harm.

Our church failed at this most fundamental human duty. The most vulnerable of all humans, defenseless children, were harmed in our care. Not only that, it took outsiders like the media and legal system to render our accountability failures transparent to us and to spur us to implement the building blocks of greater accountability going forward.

Here's a sad irony: "accountability" should be a beautiful and important word for us Catholics, because accountability is intimately linked to our vision of what human dignity entails and indispensable to living out our calling to be good stewards. Yet, at least for the moment, it has become an ugly word. One Catholic media outlet publishes an ongoing "Accountability" report, which concerns only one topic: the global church's ongoing responses to its sexual abuse crisis.

We will become more accountable, not only for those who will be entrusted to our care going forward, but in everything that concerns our mission. As we'll see, an accountable mindset is fundamentally part of the Christian worldview, and recovering that mindset will be essential to the success of our EASTeR project. We will only thrive in this confusing century if we have robust, systematic ways of assessing whether we are successfully executing the mission the Lord has given us.

This chapter is about imagining ourselves as a more accountable church. That will entail changing our practices, but, more fundamentally, changing our culture radically. In more than a few parishes, ministries, and even diocesan offices, our practices implicitly send this message: because we are involved in God's work, worldly standards of professionalism and accountability don't apply to us. In our new culture of leadership, we will start sending a very different message to the world: the principles of human dignity and good stewardship call for the very highest standards of professionalism, transparency, and accountability in all we do. We will role model those standards not only for the success of our mission but as a moral example to the rest of the world. We will no longer be perceived as laggards but as role models.

We should settle for nothing less. After all, everything in this book is posited on Jesus's vision and values, and Jesus has lots to say about accountability. "Every one to whom much is given, of him will much be required" (Luke 12:48): that straightforward teaching summarizes our Lord's theology of accountability. There are consequences to how we use our gifts. The Son of Man will one day return, and "he will sit on his glorious throne. Before him will be gathered all the nations" (Matt. 25: 31–33). Everyone who has ever attended Sunday school knows what comes next: "he will separate them one from another as a shepherd separates the sheep from the goats." Those of us who fed the hungry and welcomed the stranger will inherit eternal life. And those who didn't? Well, you know. We will be held accountable for the choices we make during our earthly sojourn.

Another parable reinforces the theme. Before departing on a long journey, the master temporarily entrusts property to his servants, "to one he gave five talents, to another two, to another one." We all know how that story ends too. One servant invests the five talents cleverly, makes five more, and is rewarded upon the master's return. But another servant buries the one talent instead of investing it; he was afraid of incurring a loss; he returns the one talent to the master and is called "wicked and slothful" (Matt. 25: 15, 26).

Doesn't it seem harsh? After all, the guy hadn't frittered away the money on booze and gambling. He was afraid and wanted to assure that the master received his original capital back. I get that. I would have cut the guy some slack. But Jesus, apparently, holds us accountable to a higher standard, not merely preserving what we've been given but growing it.

The Catholic Church has crafted an exquisitely calibrated regimen to reinforce this theology of accountability. The Ten Commandments are only a jumping-off point: we've outlined gradations of venial and mortal sin, and Catholics are urged to examine their consciences nightly. If we find ourselves wanting, we celebrate a sacrament of reconciliation that lifts sin's soul-sullying stains. In fact, confession may be the most exquisitely structured accountability ritual proposed by any religion: I own my sins, name them, pronounce remorse, pledge amends, and, astoundingly, am completely absolved.

But an ironic disconnect struck me. On the one hand, Catholic Christianity has developed an elaborate devotional and sacramental framework that helps individuals live accountably. But what about the church as a whole? We've been missioned by Jesus to make disciples, help bring God's kingdom to fruition, manifest a preferential option for poor communities, and so on: how do we know whether we are doing a good job at these mandates? How do we measure? How do we monitor whether the church is progressing or backsliding from one year to the next? What's our *institutional* accountability regime?

I couldn't find good answers. We owe it to the Lord and to our own sense of mission to become more accountable. In following paragraphs, a financial executive, a parish priest, a management consultant, three Popes, and a saint or two will help us understand how we will be better stewards, individually and institutionally, and why doing so will benefit our church immensely. They will also help us to understand how much is at stake for our church, as much as $14 billion, perhaps. That's not one time, that's annually. That's not for the whole world, but in the United States alone.

But you know something? It's not about the money, even though we will start with the financial stakes, simply because big numbers make our eyes pop: we can all imagine what $14 billion could mean to our church, and what even the tiniest slice of that could mean to our own chronically under-funded parish or ministry.

But money is only a tiny fraction of the payoff we'll realize by becoming a more accountable church: imagine the payoff that will come when we monitor whether worshippers in our parishes are spiritually nourished and growing; whether the talents of all church workers and volunteers are being recognized and promoted; whether we are reaching out to engage those who are wavering or who have drifted away; and when pastors and parishes set and track their progress toward clear, ambitious goals. The payoff for all that will be immeasurably greater than a paltry $14 billion.

## THESE HANDS CAN FIX THIS

I interviewed Monica in the city center office tower where she works as a senior executive who advises multinational companies. Sounds vague, I know. But she didn't want her story to become a "look at me" production (Monica is not her real name). Anyway, the story's point is not her case study but for you and I to understand accountability better.

Any Catholic who reads a newspaper has become painfully aware of headlines like this one from the *Financial Times*: "The Scandal at the Vatican Bank." Another periodical reported on the bank in language usually reserved for drug cartels or corrupt dictators, writing of "murky finances," at an institution that "has been accused by international regulatory bodies of turning a blind eye to money laundering, tax evasion, hidden sources of income, and other abuses."

Monica read such stories, too, and thought, "I know how to fix this." As she continues her story, she starts to sound maternal, not like an aloof financial executive. She holds out her hands, palms up, almost as if she's holding a baby: "These hands know how to fix this. It was almost that physical a feeling. There are so many things in the church that I don't have the skills to do. But this I can do. I can help." The Vatican bank's problems exactly fit her professional expertise at probing financial accounts and implementing robust risk management protocols.

She had the skills, but not a foot in the door. She tried to contact Vatican officials and heard nothing, until she was at short notice invited to explain her firm's services. And then? Not so long after, she found herself eating breakfast in the Vatican cafeteria one morning, when the Pope walked in, one of those moments when you wonder if it's all happening or a nutty dream.

I asked her what had most struck her about being involved in the Vatican's financial recovery project. "They really, really mean it," she said, "They mean to shine a light on what's not working right and make things better." An anecdote convinces me that she's not spinning me with propaganda. When Monica's forensic accounting team showed up, no conference room in the Vatican bank's cramped offices could accommodate them.

So the lay executive that Pope Benedict XVI had appointed to head the Vatican bank's reform escorted Monica into his spacious Renaissance parlor-office, told her he didn't need so much space for himself, and decamped to a relative broom closet of an office down the hall. If this guy cares so much about the mission and so little about his own ego or perks, I thought, then, yes, he means it. He wants accountability, starting with himself.

Monica's inherited office was spare of decoration save a famous painting of the gospel scene where Pharisees try to trip up Jesus by asking whether Jewish law permits payment of taxes to Caesar. The painting depicts the next moment, where Jesus holds aloft a coin with Caesar's image and says: "Render to Caesar what is Caesar's, and to God what is God's." The Jesus of that painting stared at her whenever she looked up from her work, and Monica told me, "the message I took away from it was: protect what belongs to God. That's what I felt I was there to help do."

Protect what belongs to God. We didn't create the world; God did. Nor do we own the church; it's God's. We're just temporary stewards, a notion that surfaces constantly in scripture, starting with page one of my Bible, where God instructs Adam to tend the garden. So look around your parish, school, or other ministry as if you were the metaphorical Adam, charged with tending one of God's gardens. And start to ask yourself the questions that a good steward would ask: are we using the money well? If our church worship services are boring or dreadful, are we doing something to make them better? If one-time congregants have been drifting away, what are we doing to engage our lost or alienated sheep?

Many readers will feel it's not their place to ask (and answer) such questions. That's for the pastor, for example, perhaps with input from the parish council. Sorry, but the "not my job" attitude won't fit the new culture of leadership we will now create within our church. If vital questions for our church's health are not being asked, someone has to start asking, though always in charity, always as part of the team and not as the outsider/bomb thrower, and always with the willingness to become part of a solution. Canon Law reminds us that the laity: "have the right and even at times the duty to manifest to the sacred pastors their opinion on matters which pertain to the good of the Church and to make their opinion known to the rest of the Christian faithful."

## TRANSPARENCY WILL MAKE US MORE CREDIBLE

All of which leads me back to Monica and to the practices of good stewards. Virtually none of us have the specialized financial skills to comb through Vatican financial records, so I asked what steps the rest of us could take in our own parishes, dioceses, or schools to be better stewards?

Monica pauses, as if she knows her comment will not be popular: "You know, one time, someone asked me if I thought it would be a good idea for parishes or dioceses to have something like annual shareholder meetings, similar to the way that large companies convene meetings to share financial details with shareholders and entertain questions about major decisions taken during the year. Something like that strikes me as a really good idea," she says.

I'm nodding politely, but I want to roll my eyes. Really? As if bishops and pastors don't have enough headaches already? She continues: "If we had to do that, or something like it, it would make us more transparent. And transparency immediately creates credibility: it helps secure hearts and minds; people become more trusting when they feel they know everything."

Hmm. She has a point. As she talks, I'm vaguely recalling a quote from St. John Paul II, and after my interview with her, I scurry to find it: "The church tries and will try more and more to be a 'glass house,' where all may see what is happening, and how she accomplishes her mission in fidelity to Christ." Pope Francis echoed the same idea in an address to Mexican bishops: "Do not fear transparency. The Church does not need darkness to carry out her work."

I recall an episode from my own working life, which corroborates her point about transparency and trust. I was once managing a department when the economy nosedived and we managers were instructed to cut budgets. I got ready to do what the lily-livered managerial class always does: announce the bad news in a memo and barricade my office door. But my management team pushed a different approach: why not share as much information as you can? Everyone knows that bad news is coming. Instead of presenting a *fait accompli* that leaves everyone suspicious and resentful, why not describe our situation frankly and invite input before finalizing cuts?

I wanted to do that about as much as I wanted another root canal. I envisioned myself talking to the sullen masses as they shot dagger-like stares and waited for the layoffs. But I tried the more transparent approach anyway, because I saw little to lose: it was going to be an ugly few months, however I handled it.

Well, it was as ugly as cost-cutting always is, but it also revealed the value of transparency. Subordinates were unhappy about our predicament, but most became more accepting after seeing the facts for themselves. And, while it had been "Chris's problem" before I shared the information, afterward, it became "our problem." Sure, some subordinates mined the information for ammunition to attack me. But, heck, those same folks always accused me of mismanagement anyway. For many on the team, in contrast, my transparency elicited their desire to help, and they brainstormed creative cost-saving ideas that I myself would never have conceived.

Which is what Monica was getting at. Whether it happens through "stakeholder meetings" or in other ways, we want to secure the myriad benefits that blossom when a spirit of transparency takes root: greater trust blossoms; congregants become empowered to share their solutions and ideas; Catholics feel co-responsible for their church; "us and them" thinking evaporates; decision-making skills are sharpened, because, managers (or pastors or ministry leaders in this case) must, as Monica put it, "become accustomed to explaining to others why and how we decided things the way we did, and why we use money the way we did."

## MIGHT WE REAP BILLIONS?

And there's yet another payoff for turning ourselves into a more accountable, transparent church: there will be lots more money around, as Manhattan's St. Francis Xavier discovered. I was attending Mass there one Sunday when the pastor released the parish's annual report. "We want to be accountable as a parish," he said, "You deserve to know where your money goes." He introduced the parish council president, who noted that the parish was in its second year of sharing detailed rather than superficial financial information. Then came his punchline: "Last year, when I stood up here to review our financials with you for the first time, I outlined our challenges and asked for your greater generosity. I want to thank you for your response: our collections increased by 17 percent this year."

Seventeen percent? He was speaking in a year in which the stock market had been flat, and no billionaire had enrolled in the parish, as far as I know. Can you really boost your collection by 17 percent simply by being more transparent with your finances?

Well, that's what the experts say. Researchers have long puzzled over a phenomenon that is painful even to write about: Catholics are among the stingiest denominations when it comes to religious giving. The *New York Times* once surveyed the research and reported that Baptists, for example, donate about 2 percent of their household income to religious causes, the Jewish faithful give about 1.4 percent, while we Catholics rank way down the list at 0.7 percent, trailing just about everyone.

Why such a big gap? There's no one answer to that complex question, but the research attributes a chunk of it to what Xavier parish discovered: more transparency means more giving. Charles Zech, who heads Villanova University's Center for Church Management and Business Ethics, has cited research showing that Catholics "who believe they have an input into Church decision-making processes at both the parish and diocesan levels, and who consider the Church to be accountable and transparent with its finances, contribute more."

By coincidence, as I was drafting this chapter, the annual Peter's Pence collection was taken in parishes around the world. This venerable tradition generates tens of millions of dollars annually, helping the Pope "to respond to those who are suffering as a result of war, oppression, natural disaster, and disease," the US bishops' conference tells us. I can think of few more motivating causes, yet when I toggled around the Vatican website, I found absolutely no reporting on the programs supported.

How disappointing. Pope John Paul II had long ago asserted that the church was striving to be more of a "glass house, transparent and credible": Peter's Pence seems such a lost opportunity for the Vatican to have turned those words into deeds. I can't think of any other large charities, in contrast, that collect tens of millions of dollars of donor money yet post no publicly available record of how the money was used. Let's put it constructively: imagine how much more money might flow into Peter's Pence if Catholics could see the worthy ways (I presume) in which our money is being used.

Or consider this: it's estimated that American Catholics donate approximately $8 billion annually to their parishes. $8 billion would become more than $16 billion if we Catholics donated the same percentage of income as our Baptist and Methodist brothers and sisters do. Sure, a doubling of donations seems an outrageously optimistic pipe dream in the near future. But even the 17 percent increase that Xavier parish reaped would bless our precious ministries with an additional $1.4 billion.

And that's only the income side; we can realize another enormous windfall through more professional expense management practices. Fred Gluck says that we could save up to $6 billion annually if we implemented straightforward cost-saving techniques that most major companies have adopted.

That's a lot of money, so I decided to learn more about this Gluck guy. Was he some crackpot? Some lonely guy in his basement trying to get attention?

Not quite. He worked for McKinsey and Company, the vaunted consultant to the world's most prestigious companies. He didn't just work there; he ran the place. Bottom line: this guy knows what he is talking about, so it puzzled me to learn that the church had not leapt to follow up when Fred tried to catalyze discussion by publishing his cost-savings estimate in the Catholic journal *America* and later in the *Financial Times*.

So I called him. Fred had tallied a rough estimate of the US church's total spending from data on the US bishops' conference website. Then he applied the savings formula that he and his consulting colleagues would use whenever they launched a corporate expense-savings project.

But how specifically would the savings come, I pressed? I once saw a magazine cover photo of a chief executive in business attire posing with an enormous chain saw; the executive was a brutal cost-cutter who prided himself on the nickname "Chainsaw." Was I talking to "Chainsaw Fred," who envisioned mass layoffs of loyal church employees? That would not be consistent with the church's vision of human dignity.

Nothing so cruel or breathtaking. Instead, think painstaking and methodical: "You would start with a single parish or a diocese," he told me, "and I would find out what in total the church was spending on automobiles, candles, pens and paper, cleaning supplies. You name it. You have to be specific. You have to begin by gathering the facts."

And once the data were accumulated, "The real thrust is economies of scale, good financial management, and purchasing power." To translate that financial speak into simplistic language, think of supermarket shopping. You get a much better price on toilet paper by buying ten rolls instead of one. Now picture yourself bypassing the supermarket entirely, phoning the distributor or manufacturer, and saying something like: "Hi, I represent 17,000 Catholic parishes and thousands of grammar schools. Tell me the very best price at which you would sell us five million toilet paper rolls next year." Sure, I'm oversimplifying to illustrate the point. But think not just about toilet paper; think about everything from church and school supplies to investment manager fees on pension plans to—you name it.

None of the above implies that church administrators are clueless or lazy. I've met loads of smart, dedicated church professionals while writing this book. They are trying to lead, but not enough of their church colleagues are following. For example, the bishops already have a centralized purchasing arm, but one of its business development managers told me that only about a third of church entities are using it.

Frankly speaking, we can no longer afford to leave so much money and opportunity on the table. Our parishes and ministries could accomplish so much more with the additional funds that we might generate by better donation and expense management. Let's be grateful to our ancestors in the faith, the men and women who built our schools, parishes, and hospitals through hard work and great imagination. But let's be worthy successors by stewarding these resources more conscientiously during our own Catholic generation. Could we fully close the giving gap with other denominations and generate an additional $8 billion in annual giving? Could we generate an additional $6 billion by more disciplined financial management? Maybe not. But even 1 percent of that enormous opportunity equates to $140 million, and even that is surely an opportunity worth seizing on behalf of God's people.

Let's foster the accountable mindset that spurs us to find that first 1 percent, and then the next 1 percent, always on behalf of the Lord and our ministries. And let's bring that good steward mindset to everything else we do: determined also to keep making our homilies and liturgies 1 percent more enriching, our service to poor communities ever more effective, and so on.

Put differently, let's never accept that the *status quo* is the best we can do on the Lord's behalf. Rather, we will transform our church by committing to continuous improvement in every aspect of our mission. The transformation won't come overnight; it will come 1 percent at a time, and then 2 percent at a time as we build momentum and gain confidence. The researchers who put together the highly regarded *Good to Great*, for example, found that mediocre organizations transformed themselves into great ones precisely by continuous, incremental improvement, "step by step, action by action, decision by decision," as author Jim Collins put it. The progress may not seem momentous at first, but the researchers noted "tremendous power" in the steadfast commitment to keep improving.

## THE REAL OPPORTUNITY HAS NOTHING TO DO WITH MONEY

I hope that readers were agitated on at least two counts while reading the paragraphs above. First count: *why aren't we further along already? Why are we not more diligent in pursuing these opportunities!* Second count: *I can't do anything about the Vatican bank or a national purchasing program: tell me how I can get in the game? What can I do to promote accountable stewardship in the church?*

Perfect question. Every Catholic can play a role. After all, the essence of accountability boils down to common sense. Many of us lead families or play responsible roles at our work: the first step is nothing more than manifesting similar conscientiousness for our church family as for our nuclear family, and bringing the same spirit of professionalism to our church as to our work. That's half the battle. For the rest, many resources exist. My friend Kerry Robinson, for example, heads the National Leadership Roundtable on Church Management, which promotes global "standards of excellence" for managing finances, human resources, fundraising, and other areas. That playbook can guide any parish, school, or ministry toward greater professionalism and accountability. When even ten million Catholics, less than 1 percent of us globally, take active interest in this area, we will become world class in our accountability and professionalism standards within a couple of years, I bet. That's an exciting prospect, and entirely within reach.

Importantly, those standards deal with far more than finances, because money is only a tiny sliver of the treasure and talent that God has entrusted to us. This chapter began by recalling the precious children who were abused in our care, a colossal failure of leadership and accountability at multiple levels. As Bishop James V. Johnston, Jr. of the Diocese of Kansas City–St. Joseph put it during a 2016 Service of Lament, it was not only that the abuse itself was "sinful and terrible," but it was "the response of the Church that provides a most dire cause for confession. We at times failed to act; to respond with urgency and integrity. We betrayed your trust."

At that same service, Bishop Johnston resolved to create a "visible, permanent reminder . . . a special place where we honor the stories of the past." That's really important. But let's also envision a living, future-oriented memorial, namely a fierce resolve to be more accountable in all that we do. Yes, of course we will guard the safety of those who are entrusted to us. But we will be similarly conscientious on behalf of all others whom we engage. How do we know, for example, that we are doing as good a job as we should be at helping parishioners to grow spiritually, or that we are adequately reaching out to the lost sheep who have drifted away? Do we conscientiously assess the effectiveness of our outreach to all these? As an auditor friend of mine puts it: "I believe strongly that you have to verify that you're actually doing what your documents say you're doing."

Consider a pointed example, concerning our mission to poor communities. I once attended a national conference where the archbishop of a large diocese proclaimed that, "The poor have a primary claim on [the church's] resources and concern. They are at the head of the line." I was touched and proud to belong to a church that champions that vision. But I couldn't help but wonder: how do we *know* that we are really living this vision? If, for example, we compared our church's total investment in ministries that serve poor communities against everything else we spend, from cathedral repairs to ongoing parish expenses in well-off neighborhoods, would we feel justified to say, "Yes, Lord, we've examined our conscience (and assessed our budgets!) and can tell you that the poor do indeed have the 'primary claim' on our resources. We're not just preaching it; we're doing it."

Or take another example. A prominent Cardinal not long ago wrote to his flock that, "The Church loves, welcomes, and respects a woman or man with a same-sex attraction." He went on to mention other groups that often feel marginalized, like couples living together outside marriage. I know that this high-ranking prelate meant exactly what he said. But a spirit of accountability would move us to ask ourselves: gee, do these marginalized folks actually *feel* welcome? Have we ever checked with them? Have we ever reviewed whether our outreach actually measures up to our professed welcome? Let's face it: those who feel marginalized by our church are typically not reading church newspapers: if we want them to receive our message of welcome, we'll probably have to reach out to deliver it, even if that will at first feel uncomfortable on both sides.

Central to our new culture of leadership will be the ongoing commitment to ask such questions and to develop the ever-refined skills and methods for answering them. We cannot merely profess ourselves accountable and professional; we will demonstrate it. W. Edwards Deming, the engineer and consultant who inspired the "Total Quality" movement in corporations, is credited with a quip that encapsulates the accountability mindset: "In God we trust; all others bring data." A bit irreverent, perhaps, but apt. In God we trust: God instructed us to love and serve our neighbors, and we trust God's commands on faith. But how well are we executing God's commands? We are human, not God; we will "bring data" to show that our deeds match our words.

## Good Stewards Hold Themselves Accountable

Right now, we're a bit stuck. We don't ask the questions, so we don't have the information to say whether things are going well or poorly, thus we can't really hold ourselves accountable. And if we're not holding ourselves accountable, we're not being good stewards. It's that simple.

If words like accountability, stewardship, and professionalism sound too sterile, please pray over the words of Avedis Donabedian, hailed as the founder of quality studies in health care, who once put it this way: "The secret to quality is love." It's not ultimately about tracking numbers but about showing conscientious care for the human beings whom we serve, who work for us, or who donate to us. It's about respecting them enough to role model the professionalism and excellence that befits their human dignity. It's about loving our neighbors in deeds.

So how will we get from where we are now to where we need to be? Here's the great news: God has blessed the church with all the human talent we could ever need, whether to implement robust financial management techniques or to assess whether our worship services are really helping congregants to grow closer to Jesus. All we have to do is ask our talented Catholics for help.

Healthy organizations know and make use of all the talent at their disposal; we will get better at this. I know of no diocese or parish, for example, that systematically inventories the talents of those who walk in and out of the church each Sunday: the lawyers, health care professionals, bankers, marketers, communications professionals, website developers, writers, gardeners, designers, and so on. Our bishops and parishes can lead the effort to catalogue the abundant talents that God has bestowed on the church and, importantly, create more space and opportunity for all these Catholics to share their gifts. As Pope John Paul II once instructed a group of American bishops: "a commitment to creating better structures of participation, consultation and shared responsibility . . . [is] an intrinsic requirement of the exercise of episcopal authority." Let's steward well the skills of dedicated Catholics who might help us steward all else in the church.

But it's not only those with hierarchical authority who need to role model better accountability. So do the rest of us. Only when both sides act will the church attain Pope Benedict XVI's vision that, "the co-responsibility of all the members of the People of God in their entirety is gradually promoted," so that laypeople are "truly recognized as 'co-responsible' for the Church's being and action." This chapter's message? Such words will remain more hallucination than vision until we all strive, both top-down and bottom-up, to bring them alive.

Monica gives us this chapter's closing image. She read about the church's financial travails and felt, almost palpably: "These hands can help fix this." That goes equally for the rest of us: each person's hands will help fix this. Each, by virtue of baptism, is called to help fix this. Everyone leads.

We'll manifest that leadership by becoming more accountable and entrepreneurial and by channeling our energies toward three shared priorities: wet socks, the glow, and dusty shoes. What might those vivid but mystifying images mean? They represent three critical priorities for the EASTeR project and are elaborated in following chapters.

## *Pray, Reflect, Discuss, and Act*

- For individuals and small groups: Are you holding yourself(ves) sufficiently accountable in your parish, work, or ministry? Does your parish or ministry have ways of monitoring whether you are succeeding in your mission, and whether parishioners are growing as disciples? How could you be more transparent with congregants and stakeholders in ways that might build further trust and "co-responsibility" for the mission?

- For parishes and other ministries: Adopt the Leadership Roundtable's "standards of excellence," or some other program, to guide your parish or ministry to proven best practices in human resources, finance, administration, and other functions.

- For dioceses and nationally: Undertake a "John Paul II Glass House Project," that is, identify specific opportunities to show greater transparency, build trust, and generate shared ownership for mission.

- For the national church: Convene a "billion for God's billion" task force of finance and operations experts who will, within 180 days, recommend concrete steps that would enable the church to optimize its purchasing and expense management practices, targeting $1 billion in annual savings. Donate the first billion dollars in savings to Catholic Relief Services, Caritas, or other church programs that benefit the billion poorest people on earth.

# CHAPTER EIGHT

# Wet Socks

## *A Church That Serves All in Need*

THERE IS SOMETHING OF PATRICIA INSIDE EVERY ONE OF US. AND whenever it blossoms, it changes our church and changes the world.

A famous Dickens line ran through my mind as I listened to her story: "it was the best of times; it was the worst of times." She used to take the train to downtown Philadelphia for a part-time job at Bonwit Teller, the most fashionable store on the most prosperous shopping street in America's third-largest city. Heady stuff for a teenager who had not even reached legal working age. "I modeled," but she adds modestly, "not anything big-time." She must have cut a graceful figure in those Bonwit dresses: she was also an aspiring ballet and tap dancer.

Which gets to why that idyllic teenaged life was also, in a sense, the worst of times. See, she only got her chance to work at Bonwit because "the manpower shortage was still on." It was 1944; many of Philadelphia's employment-age men were soldiers in World War II. And many of the women who might otherwise have worked at Bonwit Teller were instead laboring where Philadelphia's men typically would, in factories that churned out machine parts and munitions. With women in factory jobs, children like Patricia got to work in fancy stores like Bonwit.

Her modeling career was not the only chance that war afforded her: "I used to dance at the St. Benedict's Catholic USO [the United Service-man's Organization]. That was for the soldiers and sailors and marines. I also started to dance at the Rush hospital, which had been turned into a place for wounded servicemen. I had seen them young and handsome and vigorous in 1943, and then I was seeing a lot of wounded." Decades later, she still remembers some of the faces.

I was touched to hear that story, even though I couldn't make out how it related to the question I had first asked her about her current calling. But then the story took a turn that explained both her life's work and her place at the head of this chapter. When she was a high school senior, a nun asked her to conduct a weekend dance workshop at a Catholic grammar school that was some distance away. "During the visit, I stayed in the convent for two days. That gave me a chance to look at convent life somewhat from the inside. And I had wondered sometimes if a religious vocation was for me. And some time after that weekend, I did decide to enter." That's how Patricia, part-time model and ballet dancer, became Sr. Rita Scully. File that story under, "God works in mysterious ways."

A teaching career unfurled from that weekend, including at suburban Philadelphia's Chestnut Hill College, where I first met her. She teaches literature and writing, but every once in a while gets to reprise her dancing days. When a student dance club wanted to re-create dances from the time of the college's founding, Sr. Rita was drafted to teach the Charleston. Sr. Rita was well into her sixties then: I hope I am half as spry at that age.

## WET SOCKS: A KEY TO THE CHURCH'S FUTURE

Or even a fraction as spry as she is now, which gets to this story's point. Not long ago, she took on a new challenge. She still loves to travel to downtown Philly, just as in her teenaged years. But nowadays, she typically does so on her way to Saturday evening Mass at a picturesque church that is a few decades older than the United States itself, Old St. Joseph's.

One day, as she was dipping a hand into the holy water font to bless herself, a woman sidled over and offered some unsolicited advice: "You know, I don't touch the holy water in any of the city's churches any more, ever since I saw a homeless person rinsing out a pair of filthy socks in a holy water font."

I guess I would have recoiled from the font. But that wasn't Sr. Rita's reaction: "I thought, well, there must be people who need socks, and there's something I can do." That's how an entrepreneur thinks: here's a need, and I can do something about it. And that's leadership: let me show the way forward instead of waiting for someone else. And that's accountability: the Lord told us to care for our brothers and sisters, and I hold myself accountable to that standard. And that's what will revitalize our church: the impulse to think first and always of loving and serving others, especially those who are marginalized by society. A new ministry was born at that holy water font. What perfect symbolism—at the spot where we recall our baptism, Sr. Rita found a new way to live out her baptismal call to lead.

"I started from then to buy pairs of socks," she goes on, "and put each pair in a plastic bag, and then I also put in the bag a list of the places where a homeless person can get a meal." I didn't quite get it: did she drop off her little baggie with the socks at a homeless shelter or a soup kitchen? Nothing so impersonal for Sr. Rita. Rather, whenever she takes the train into central Philly to attend Mass, she says, "I come out at 12th and Market Streets; I start walking, and I stop whenever I see a homeless person on the street." She usually carries three pairs of socks, each neatly packaged in its own little bag, each with the list of places where meals and job referrals are available. I ask how far she gets before depleting her sock inventory: "usually by about the time I get to 9th and Market." That's three blocks, about one homeless person per block.

Sr. Rita was nearing her eighty-sixth birthday when she told me that story. She seems pretty fit, though perhaps no longer spry enough for the Charleston. And she's petite; I doubt if she's even five feet tall. And, let's be frank, the rest of us often associate homelessness with mental illness, substance abuse, and criminality. So I wondered how this diminutive woman manages her encounters: maybe she deposits her little sock bag at a safe distance and moves along? No. "I ask the person his or her first name. I tell them I will say a prayer for them. And then I say: *And you must please say a prayer for me too, for Patricia.*" (She uses her birth name rather than her religious name when she speaks with them).

"And one time, one of them, Gary was his name, said to me: *I don't know if I know how to do that, how to pray.* So I said to him: *Well, I'm gonna say, 'God bless Gary.' And what you can say is, 'God bless Patricia.'* And Gary said: *Well, that's not hard. I guess I can do that.* And then he asks me: *I have a girlfriend, Jennifer. Do you think you could say a prayer for her?"*

During another encounter, after she asked a man to pray for her, he simply said: *"You're already blessed."*

I listen to her and recall Pope Francis's address to a group of charity workers, "Tell me, when you give alms, do you look the person in the eye? . . . [D]o you touch the hand of the person you are giving them to, or do you toss the coin at him or her." We may think we are being suitably compassionate by allowing some down-and-out person to warm up in the back of the church in winter. But I guess that's mere tolerance: they are warm, yes, but have remained anonymous outsiders, in plain sight yet somehow invisible. Sr. Rita does it the way the Pope said it ought to be done, taking the time to learn someone's name, to share her own name, and to ask for prayers, acknowledging that she too has something to receive from this person. There is mutuality in Christian relationships: we don't condescend, as if we are somehow superior.

## SEE A POOR MAN: "IMAGINE YOU BEHOLD AN ALTAR"

St. John Chrysostom, that great fourth-century doctor of the church, captures what is really happening when Sr. Rita encounters a homeless person. We venerate the altar in church, Chrysostom wrote, because, "it receives Christ's body." But that's not the only place we reverence our Lord, he continues: "whenever you see a poor man, imagine you behold an altar. When you see a beggar, don't insult him but reverence him." Or, as St. Vincent de Paul put it, "If ten times a day you go to serve persons who are poor, ten times a day you will meet God there."

As I listen to Sr. Rita, I feel a bit ashamed. She's the Good Samaritan, who tends the wounded stranger on the roadside, even at some personal risk and expense. Most days, I'm the Levite priest who bypasses the poor guy, because I'm too busy or fear being accosted. I'm skilled at rationalizing my behavior: our city offers ample resources to help the homeless, and, anyway, if I give some street person money, it would probably be wasted on drugs or alcohol.

That's worldly logic, not Jesus's logic (more on that later). We believe in a more fascinating power (more to come on that as well). And every teaspoon of fact in that rationale comes with tablespoons of knee-jerk stereotyping: I ask eighty-something Sr. Rita, for example, how often she has been accosted during hundreds of sock encounters with these big, bad, dangerous homeless people. Not once.

Sr. Rita gave me both a meditation on my feebleness and an icon for one of our twenty-first-century priorities: wet socks. Picture that misguided, forlorn vagrant plunging his dirty socks into the holy water font. That image may offend our sensibilities but reminds us what our Christian lives are about. Sr. Rita beheld in those dirty, wet socks an invitation to compassion and service. Let's make that way of thinking and acting our hallmark. What should come to mind when people think of us Christians? Oh yeah, they are the ones who love, serve, and seek justice for anyone in need.

Why? That's what Jesus told us to do. No further reason is needed. But other reasons abound. The all-encompassing commitment to serve will energize us, unite us, transform our hearts, intrigue an increasingly secular world, and attract young adults, all of which will be outlined in following paragraphs. All that and heaven too. Pope John Paul II once took stock of the world's violence, cruelty, and self-absorption and urged Christians to respond with "the fascinating power of love." Let's wield love's fascinating power more forcefully.

After all, that was one of Jesus's top priorities. He distilled all Jewish law into a straightforward command: "You shall love the Lord your God with all your heart, and with all your soul, and with all your mind. And a second is like it. You shall love your neighbor as yourself" (Matt. 22: 37–40). And, our "neighbors," Jesus taught in the parable of the Good Samaritan, are all those in need, not just those who live nearby, or who share our ethnicity or religious tradition. "[Who] proved neighbor to the man who fell among the robbers," Jesus asked. "The one who showed mercy on him," the scribe answered. And so it ought to be for all of us.

After receiving an honorary doctoral degree at Manhattan College, Cardinal Timothy Dolan said: "At the cosmic final exam, Jesus is not going to ask us about our college degree. . . . He is certainly not going to ask about a Cardinal's red hat. . . . All he is going to do is ask us . . . if we fed the hungry, if we helped heal the sick, if we clothed the naked and welcomed the stranger, if we visited the imprisoned and educated those unlearned. In other words, if selfless, sacrificial love has been our hallmark."

What if those really are life's final exam questions? What will I say when Jesus asks whether I welcomed the stranger? I thought about that uncomfortable question after hearing about what the Sisters of the Holy Redeemer are doing.

New vocations have been scarce for years for these sisters; their average age, consequently, has climbed to seventy-nine (yes: the *average*, not the age of the eldest); and their historic, centuries-old convent in Wurzburg, Germany, is now partially empty.

So the city government asked whether the sisters would devote space to accommodating some of Germany's growing ranks of asylum seekers. The sisters mulled the government's request. Some sisters wondered whether they could at least vet and interview each refugee before accepting him or her (no, it doesn't work that way, they learned). Others raised practical concerns, like how would the German-speaking sisters ever communicate with their refugee guests?

Let's face it: we could all probably think of easier ways for elderly sisters to fill their extra rooms than with refugees from Afghanistan, Syria, Ukraine, and elsewhere. The logical thing would surely have been to decline politely. Who could reasonably expect these women to make themselves vulnerable and disrupt their convent's peace and daily rhythm? But the sisters didn't do the logical thing. Or, better put, they live according to a different logic, that of Jesus. They decided to wield the fascinating power of love.

Who knows, maybe they saw themselves as paying back an old favor. After all, we Christians trace our lineage to an impoverished, refugee family. We see cherubic Jesus in his manger and three wise men offering gold, frankincense, and myrrh. But recall what happens right after that idyllic moment—an angel appears to Joseph in a dream, and instructs him, "Rise, take the child and his mother, and flee to Egypt, and remain there till I tell you; for Herod is about to search for the child, to destroy him" (Matt. 2:13).

Who sheltered the Holy Family each night during their weeklong journey into Egypt? Who took them in during that stay in Egypt, which might have lasted as long as two years? The scriptures don't tell us, but we can be sure that Joseph, a poor carpenter, wasn't whipping out a credit card and staying in high-end hotels. He likely begged for food and lodging, just as today's refugees sometimes must. Presumably, Egyptian families sheltered Jesus from the violent threat back home, just as these German sisters have shown similar mercy to Syrians who are fleeing barrel bombs and the other mayhem wrought by Syria's civil war.

## Christ Has No Hands but Ours

Sr. Simone Rollman is one of the refugees' hosts, one of the seventy-somethings who serve meals to refugee families, prepare rooms for new arrivals, help them to navigate government bureaucracies, and accompany them through discouragement. Why does she do it? Her answer comes in the straightforward style one associates with Germans: "From the Bible, 'what you have done to the least of these, you have done to me,' and from our congregation's patroness St. Teresa of Avila: 'Christ has no hands but yours.'"

She is Christ's hands for these refugees, sure, but I also wondered how her seventy-something legs were holding up and how her German tongue communicated with Syrians and Afghans. Just fine, apparently: "I only speak German, but I believe that there is also another language that we all know: speaking with our hands and feet and using our hearts and our intuition. Some might say that I am too old for this but for me age plays no role when I am at the right place, involved in God's mission."

Anyway, don't worry about Sr. Simone; this is how she sums up her days: "I am doing what fills my heart with love." How many of us get the chance to say that at age seventy-four, or at any age for that matter? Now that I think about it, in a consumer culture that typically peddles the superficial and ephemeral, I can't imagine a more appealing pitch for our Christian promise than Sr. Simone's: join us and do what will fill your heart with love.

So Sr. Simone is feeling great, but how about her refugee guests? Hassan (not his real name) is a Syrian who temporarily lived in the convent with his wife and three children. He had been shuffled from one refugee camp to another before learning that he would be sent to a religious complex that he could only conceptualize as a "church," an unwelcome surprise for this devout Muslim. But soon, he says, "we understood that the place is a friendly place and full of peace. We see that the Sisters are very old but do their best to make sure that people from different countries live here together in peace. They make us feel like a family. We can only be thankful for their love, humanity, and selflessness. They are patient even when the children are noisy and messy."

He shared his observations about other refugees: "We see the changes that this place makes in us and in others coming here. We become more peaceful inside. Sometimes people who come here are angry after all that they have experienced but after a few days here, we see a change in them. They become more quiet. . . . [The sisters] are like mothers to all of us, not just the children but us adults, too. Sometimes we ask ourselves how can the Sisters be like this? They always smile, always help, always are patient—it must be their education in the church that makes them this way."

Fatma, not her real name, also lived there, together with her husband and son. Like Hassan, she had been warehoused in a large camp: "It was awful. We had no rest, there was a lot of stress and we always felt angry." And now with the sisters? "Here, everything is peaceful. We feel like we are in a family, not in a camp. We feel human again. I am Muslim but I believe that we and the Sisters have one God. Before the war in Syria, it was normal that people of different faiths were friends. . . . The war separated us and we became afraid of each other. . . . With the Sisters, we are all one family again."

Who would not be touched by testimonies like this? But let's take a step back and imagine that we had been advisors to seventy-four-year-old Sr. Simone or eighty-six-year-old Sr. Rita, our "wet socks" sister. Surely we would have tried to dissuade them from inviting refugees into their convent home or approaching homeless persons on the street. We would have marshalled plenty of logical arguments why these senior citizens should not be exposing themselves to the risks.

Plenty of politicians say likewise. A respected American presidential candidate once argued that the country should accept only the refugees it "needs," those who can "boost our economy." A European prime minister argued against accepting refugees who "have been raised in another religion, and represent a radically different culture."

## THE FASCINATING POWER OF LOVE

Hmm. Let's be grateful that those Egyptians who sheltered the Holy Family didn't think like our modern politicians, because the refugee Holy Family was not "needed" and did not "boost the economy" either. Granted, there's logic to accepting only those refugees who "boost the economy," but there's nothing particularly Christian in that self-interested mindset. Jesus told us to feed the hungry and welcome the stranger not because they will pay us back, boost our economy, join our church, or vote for our party. That's why Pope John Paul II called Christian charity "the fascinating power of love," precisely because it transcends worldly logic, self-interest, and even, at times, plain old common sense.

That may feel radical. It is. Blame Jesus, not me. If we do good only to those who do good to us, Jesus said, "what credit is that to you? For even sinners do the same" (Luke 6:33). He tells us to "love your enemies, and do good, and lend, expecting nothing in return." Imitate God the Father, who is "kind to the ungrateful and the selfish" (Luke 6:35). And whenever we're tempted to look down on those who were victims not of bad luck or injustice but of their own laziness, irresponsibility, and bad choices, Jesus says this: "Judge not, and you will not be judged; condemn not, and you will not be condemned" (Luke 6:37).

Here's how Jesus sums up his illogical manifesto about the fascinating power of love: "Love your enemies, do good to those who hate you, bless those who curse you . . . from him who takes away your cloak, do not withhold your coat as well. Give to everyone who begs from you" (Luke 6: 27–30).

The logical reaction to those wet socks would be to enhance security so that vagrants cannot sully our holy water font; the Christian reaction is to seek solutions to homelessness and poverty. And Jesus-logic may prove our best chance to intrigue a jaded twenty-first-century culture. The world grows increasingly self-absorbed, acquisitive, consumerist, individualistic, and Darwinian. We will be the fascinating opposite of that, with an identity that really sets us apart.

Thank God for Sr. Simone, Sr. Rita, and countless other Christians like them. They are leading the way for the rest of us, pointing to a vision of what our church can and should be. Just think, for example, if the whole world spoke of us just as the refugees speak of those sisters: "they make us feel like a family. We can only be thankful for their love, humanity and selflessness. . . . They are like mothers to all of us . . . they always smile, always help . . . [their place] is a friendly place and full of peace."

What's more, these sisters were evangelizing through their loving service; that is, those refugees perceived clearly that religious faith had inspired the sisters' loving deeds. As Hassan saw it, "it must be their education in the church that makes them this way." We Catholics could have no better "brand" than that of these sisters, and they won it not by slick advertising but simply by manifesting the fascinating power of love.

Let's follow their lead, because we need some brand rehabilitation. I once heard a homily by Bishop James McElroy, then an auxiliary bishop in San Francisco. He told of a retreat where young adult Catholic leaders had gathered to brainstorm approaches for drawing more of their young adult peers to the faith. At the outset, the bishop asked these leaders to discuss their peers' perceptions of the church. After working in small groups for a while, the retreatants presented their findings. The two words that summarized their friends' take on the Catholic Church? "Distant" and "judgmental."

Think about it. The refugees found the sisters, "selfless, patient, and full of peace." In contrast, these young adults, many of them after years of Catholic formation, found us "distant and judgmental." Something has gone seriously wrong here. It makes me feel like doing what the prophet Mordecai did: "[he] rent his clothes and put on sackcloth and ashes, and went out into the midst of the city, wailing with a loud and bitter cry" (Esth. 4:1). These young people are our church's future, and every survey confirms that we're letting them slip away from us.

We don't have to. Yes, young adults may profess an ever-diminishing interest in organized religion, but they are not immune to the fascinating power of love. In fact, they are downright enthusiastic about Jesus's call to serve poor communities and to champion social justice causes. That was a research finding about young adults, published in *American Catholics*

*Today*. First some bad (but unsurprising news): only 27 percent of young adults regard the Church's teaching authority as crucial in their vision of Catholicism; they want to make up their own minds about moral issues. We can rub their noses into the Church's teaching authority as much as we like; that might make us feel righteous, but it won't likely win their attention or change their minds.

## HOW TO CATCH THE MODERN WORLD'S ATTENTION

But there's good news: what if we engage them by inviting them to serve alongside us in the church-run homeless shelter? A whopping 91 percent of young adults surveyed saw "helping the poor" as crucial to Catholicism; that was a substantially higher percentage than for older Catholics. We serve the needy and advocate for justice because that's what Jesus told us to do. But how encouraging that our commitment to the poor might also be the ticket to engaging young adults in the church more generally.

It's just as Pope Paul VI once said: "Modern man listens more willingly to witnesses than to teachers, and if he does listen to teachers, it is because they are witnesses." So let's redouble our witness to charity and justice. Ironically, our best hope of engaging the twenty-somethings is to imitate those seventy-somethings and eighty-somethings, Sisters Simone and Rita.

And our witness to charity and justice might also become our most powerful evangelization outreach. Think of the world in which our earliest Christian ancestors lived, an environment indifferent and often hostile to the Jesus movement. But love swayed that empire. The Emperor Julian the Apostate, for example, ascended to power a few decades after Constantine instituted tolerance for Christians. But Julian's malevolence toward Christianity was as strong as Constantine's benevolence had been. Julian rebuilt pagan temples and restored polytheism to the Empire's forefront. But Julian brandished cleverness, not fury: instead of throwing Christians to the lions, he stockpiled pagan temples with bread.

Huh? Well, as Julian saw it, Christianity was rapidly winning adherents at paganism's expense, because Christians "support not only their poor, but ours as well, all men see that our people lack aid from us." As

Julian saw it, "it is their benevolence to strangers, their care for the graves of the dead and the pretended holiness of their lives that have done most to increase [Christianity]." His tactical conclusion was straightforward: "I believe that we [i.e., the pagans] ought really and truly to practise every one of these virtues." Instead of martyring Christians, therefore, Julian resolved to compete by emulating Christians. Thus, this enemy of Christianity has unwittingly offered one of history's more eloquent testimonies on Christianity's behalf.

Could our charitable witness today be just as effective in winning the interest and hearts of a secular society? Pope Benedict XVI sure thought so: "Living charity is the primary form of missionary outreach," he wrote, "The word proclaimed and lived becomes credible if it is incarnate in behaviour that demonstrates solidarity and sharing, in deeds that show the Face of Christ as man's true Friend."

And Pope Benedict also reminds us that we are called not only to charitable deeds but to pursue justice for all who lack it. Yes, we serve by feeding the hungry, but we also serve by asking *why* people are hungry, homeless, poorly educated; or why they lack clean water, adequate health care, or access to dignified working conditions. Once upon a time, we Christians shied from such questions. As Brazil's late Bishop Dom Helder Câmara once famously put it: "When I feed the poor, they call me a saint. When I ask why so many people are poor, they call me a communist."

But Pope Benedict XVI defined our duty unambiguously: "[T]hanks to the Magisterium . . . it has become clearer to all of us that justice and charity are the two inseparable aspects of the single social commitment of Christians. . . . It is incumbent on lay faithful in particular to work for a just order in society."

We will serve the needy, through charity *and* by seeking a more just world, because our eternal life depends on it, because it will unify us as a church, because it will engage our teenagers and young adults, and because it will fascinate the wider world as it once did the Roman Empire. But it will also do something else: it will transform our own hearts and lives, as we rediscover anew a great mystery of Christian life: "give, and it will be given to you" (Luke 6:38). As Jesus put it, "Whoever loses his life for my sake will find it" (Matt. 17: 24–25). Consider how true that's been of Sr. Simone, for example. She gave up her privacy, leisure time, security, and some of her community's possessions; yet her work, she said, "fills my heart with love." She has been transformed. She has given, but she has received more.

I regularly encountered that phenomenon while researching this chapter. I had been bumbling along according to my own worldly logic, searching for stories of those whose lives had been transformed by receiving Christian charity. I instead found stories of lives that had been transformed by *bestowing* charity. Take Sr. Simone, for example, whose seventy-four-year-old "heart is full of love." Or take Kaylin House Murphy, an Arkansas nurse who tells of a very early morning when she was doing the juggling act that all great nurses master: moving as expeditiously as possible from one hospital room to the next, yet all the while trying to bestow reverent care on each patient.

After tending to one blind woman, before whirling to leave the room she asked whether her patient needed anything more. "Yes," the woman replied, "Is the sun rising yet?" That stopped Kaylin in her tracks. She had been too busy even to notice. So she went over and peeked through a window blind before replying, "Yes, ma'am it is."

At the old woman's request, the nurse opened the blinds fully. The woman told her story, that of a young girl who had long ago lost her sight in an accident. The nurse watched tears trickle from the sightless eyes of a now elderly woman who wished she could behold one more sunrise. So Kaylin took the woman's hand and painted a verbal picture, of shadows lifting, of golden rays, and of orange, grey, and purple hues. The patient, now smiling through tears, thanked her for describing what the sighted so often take for granted.

Then something unexpected happened. Or, more accurately, something else unexpected happened. The woman gave her a little sermonette, "Most people worry about tomorrow. They don't stop to see the beauty God has put in front of them, or the promises of beauty within that prove God's love. So I ask you, who is it that is truly blind? If God takes care of the birds, don't you think God will take care of you? I depend on God every day to take care of me. Today, God sent a young girl to describe a sunrise to me. If you open your eyes, you will see that God will take care of you, too."

Now it was the nurse's turn to cry. She later wrote: "I realized that healing had taken place for both of us. . . . I was being robbed by worry, fear and doubt, when, in fact, each day was a blessing." Many mornings, since then, she wrote, when she sees the sunrise, "I think of my patient and thank God for sending her across my path."

Who will we be as a church in the twenty-first century? We will be the wet socks people, the ones who intrigue the world by the fascinating power of love. We will be the church that is known for love and service to anyone in need, and for championing a more just world.

And our hearts and souls will be transformed in the process, as we will discover next.

## Pray, Reflect, Discuss, and Act

- Pray over and discuss Sr. Rita's "wet socks" story: have you similarly had moments where some opportunity to love and serve has become equally palpable? Can you conceive one small act of Christian service that you could undertake tomorrow?

- Are the poor really "at the head of the line"? Annually assess (within your personal life, the parish, or other ministry) the proportion of time, ministerial effort, or budget that is directed toward poor and vulnerable communities. Find ways to increase that proportion annually.

- For bishops: convene representatives of the diocese's parishes, hospitals, schools, social service agencies, and poor communities to assess how well the local church, in all its ministries taken together, is serving under-served communities and how it could do better.

CHAPTER NINE

# The Glow

## *A Church That Transforms Hearts and Souls*

8,607,685.

That number ought to haunt every Catholic, yet no reader will recognize it.

Admittedly, the number is not nearly so precise as I suggest, but the accurate number would be far greater than eight million. Some 13 percent of Americans, as many as forty million people, consider themselves "former Catholics," according to Pew Research. How discouraging. If "former Catholicism" were a religion, it would be America's second largest.

But let's consider only one subset of that forty million: many of these former Catholics now worship at other Christian churches, and 71 percent of such folks say that they left our church because, "my spiritual needs were not being met." By my *very* rough math, that works out to more than 8 million people.

What on earth is our church here for if not to "meet the spiritual needs" of the baptized? And those eight million are only the tip of the iceberg of spiritually unfulfilled Catholics. Look around church next Sunday and you'll surely see at least a few folks who look pretty disengaged. But at least they are showing up: more than 75 percent of US Catholics don't even bother to attend Mass regularly. We're hardly meeting their spiritual needs if the Sunday crossword puzzle seems more worthwhile to them than Sunday worship. Bottom line? The fallen away, the disengaged attendees, and the stay-at-homes add up to the great majority of baptized Catholics, a vast population whose spiritual needs are not being met. It's time for soul searching and action.

A few readers may object that these opening paragraphs have it backward: it's not about meeting *your* spiritual needs; it's about your duty to praise and reverence *God*. Stop focusing on yourself, these readers might argue, like some "feverish selfish little clod of ailments and grievances complaining that the world will not devote itself to making you happy," in George Bernard Shaw's delicious words.

Sorry, that critique is off base, because as this chapter will make clear, when folks talk about their spiritual needs, they're not referring to the "me" stuff like entertaining Masses with coffee klatches afterward. Rather, they want to draw closer to Jesus, to understand the gospel better, and to be challenged in their faith; they want inner peace, deep meaning, and a sense of community. They want the very things that our church promises to offer. Judging by the numbers, we're not fulfilling our mission as well as we should be. We need to hold ourselves more accountable to that disheartening fact and become more entrepreneurial in seeking ways to improve.

Hence this chapter. We will become a church where hearts and souls are always transformed, where individuals are converted into closer disciples of Jesus. How do we get better at doing that? I started by asking Beatrice, and Beatrice led me to an even better source: the Holy Spirit.

## MEETING BEATRICE: IN SEARCH OF "THE GLOW"
I first met Beatrice when I . . .

Only after starting that sentence did I realize that I could not finish it. Not because I lack the facts. Beatrice had narrated a life story that was alternately horrific and beautiful, and she seemed buoyed throughout by an inner peace that never deserted her.

Except once. Not because I had probed indelicately into some unpleasant episode but when I asked an innocuous question, "Could you spell your last name for me?" Only then did it fully dawn on her that her name would appear in a book. She glanced away, as if hoping the question would go away. But it hung in the air between us. She must have felt embarrassed. She had agreed to tell her story for my book: how could she not have realized that telling your story involves telling your name?

Well, given what she has been through, she was entitled to whatever fears she harbored. I wondered what it feels like to lose one of life's most basic freedoms: that of sharing your name without fear. "Don't worry about it," I said, "I'll find a way to tell the story without telling your name, or where you live or work." She relaxed again; a cloud lifted; and "the glow" came back.

That's how I came to describe her aura of serenity; it seemed almost as visible as a "glow." I had noticed it during a first, chance meeting, as I tagged along when a friend of mine visited Beatrice. The three of us chatted for only a few minutes, which was enough for me to want to return and figure out what Beatrice has. At first, I just wanted to learn more about this intriguing person; only later did I appreciate that she embodied this chapter's theme and a key priority for revitalizing our church.

She cleans houses, though her circumstances had been far different. Once upon a time, she didn't lift a finger to clean her own house. Hired help did that for her, and hired help cooked. She was a schoolteacher in a country where teachers were highly respected; her husband, director of a secondary school, was perched atop an even higher social pedestal. They had status, and they enjoyed it.

But in the course of a short time, they lost everything: their possessions, social standing, the freedom to share their identity beyond a trusted circle, even, in a sense, their humanity. After all, if you are hunted down by predators, doesn't that make you more animal than human?

See, Beatrice is Rwandan, a survivor of the ethnic hostility that exploded most famously (and gruesomely) in those hundred days of 1994 when as many as a million Rwandans, 20 percent of the country's population, were slaughtered in what has become known as the "Rwandan genocide." Many of the hunted had cowered at home or huddled in churches until machete-wielding neighbors found and butchered them. Others survived rape or genital mutilation with knives, boiling water, or acid. Still others, once the first orgy of ethnic violence ended, became targets for revenge killings.

## Hunted Like Animals, and Finding God

What had Beatrice seen or suffered? I didn't try to drag the details from her. To what end? She lived through humanity's foremost barbarity of the late twentieth century; no one needs to read further details to become convinced of its horrors. Still, a few details trickled out. She had seen family members killed and then she fled Rwanda and sheltered in a ramshackle refugee settlement in Zaire (now Congo), until the camp itself became a hunting ground, infiltrated by militants from one side or another.

So Beatrice and her husband set off again, scrambling through forest, foraging for food, worrying that each sound in the bush was not a harmless animal but a persecutor. She remembers the occasional thwop-thwop of United Nations helicopters above, impotently monitoring the hunt that played out below. Eventually her family reached the country where I met her, arriving with the clothes on their backs, nightmarish memories, and nothing else. They took shelter where they could, slept on bare ground, begged for food, and slowly wasted away until an aid worker arranged her present housecleaning job.

So what does it do to your heart to live through all that? Her husband, at first, drew the conclusion that I pray I wouldn't but fear I might, "How can God exist when I see suffering like this. God cannot exist," she remembers him saying one afternoon as they trudged by rotting corpses.

And Beatrice herself? She pauses for a moment, tilts her head, sighs a little, and recalls life before the genocide, "I used to go to church because others go. I used to receive without knowing what I was receiving. And I didn't pray because I didn't see any significance to prayers. I had the idea of a God who is very, very far away, someone who didn't know me or my circumstances." Then came the Congo, "We were chased every day through the grass, I was seeing people dying before my eyes. Why was I still alive? I used to meditate on this question but also to doubt." Then her eyes moisten, and she recites a date, "August 21, 1999."

"Yes?"

She continues, occasionally grasping for a word in English or lapsing into her native French, but her lack of English fluency only amplifies her message. She says what's essential, without tangential flourishes: "I had a dream in which Jesus appeared and he looked at me with great compassion. And the dream gave me great peace and great thirst for him. From that day, I had the grace to pray for a long time. From that day to now, I find prayer very sweet in my heart."

I'm humbled. But I can't help being the postmodern American who believes in science and knows that the mind sometimes plays tricks. I wonder as I listen: *Did Jesus really appear to her in a dream? Or was it, well, just part of a dream?* But I'm smart enough to keep those wonders to myself. And, anyway, I'm less inclined to skeptical inquiry than to take off my shoes, because I've realized that I'm on holy ground.

But still, I can't help but think: she lived a nice life; now she cleans the rooms of people who are less educated and less successful than she herself once was. She had money; now she has virtually none. She lost everything, not through her own reckless choices, but as a victim of injustice. I imagine stewing in bitterness and resentment if something like that had happened to me. What about her? Does she feel anger? "When I came here I was very poor. I was hungry. Sometimes we slept on the floor, without a mattress. But I discovered God in my poverty. I never discovered similar joy as in my poverty. It is a different kind of joy than you have from material things. The spiritual joy is like a thirst, but it is not a painful thirst."

I've come across such phrases before, say in centuries-old, pious memoirs of saints, or from preachers who, God forgive my judgmentalism, sounded as if they were reading from a book rather than sharing lived experience. Now, I believe I'm hearing from someone who knows. Her lived experience gives her words power, just as they said of Jesus: "he speaks with authority, not like one of the scribes."

## GOD CHOOSES THE WEAK TO SHAME THE POWERFUL
Other scripture passages start rattling around my head as well. I'm looking at this diminutive, soft-spoken woman in her neat but modest attire, sitting in one of the homes she cleans, and I know that the world's "important" people would not give her the time of day, and I really get, perhaps for the first time, what St. Paul told us, "in my weakness is God made strong," and I know what Jesus meant when he said, "God chose the weak to shame the powerful."

Before we finish, she gives me occasion to recall one other scripture. It's the only time I see a tear escape her eyes, a solitary drop that slides down her left cheek and leaves a moist trail. She is talking about the person she holds accountable for the deaths of close family members, and she tells me, "I pray for him too. But it was very hard. I used to pray for him and I would say, *God, you see that what I'm praying from my lips is different than what I am feeling in my heart. Give me the strength to pray for him in love.*" It's exactly as Jesus told us: "Pray for your enemies and those who persecute you." I feel humbled that I had the chance in life to meet someone who was doing so, under those most painful possible circumstances.

In the days after our conversation, I come to realize that my silly little nickname, "the glow," wasn't silly at all. She radiated serenity, as if the "glow" emanated from within. I recalled other stories about the glow. Recall Moses, for example, who clambers up Mt. Sinai and walks back down with Ten Commandments, and: "His face shone because he had been speaking with God" (Exod. 34:29). The glow.

And what about that iconic post-Resurrection story of the two disciples on the road to Emmaus? They trudge along, downcast and bewildered, mulling Jesus's barbaric crucifixion and the incomprehensible report of resurrection. Jesus himself suddenly falls into step beside them, though they do not recognize his now-glorified body and think him a stranger. This perceived stranger breaks bread with them before continuing on his way. Only later do they realize that this stranger was, in fact, their Lord. As they put it, "did not our hurts burn within us" (Luke 24:32). The glow.

## Who Is Truly Rich?

So what does Beatrice's story have to do with the rest of us? Everything. Granted, few of us would trade places with her external circumstances, but who would not want what she has within? She is peaceful, warm, and open. She feels close to her God. We stew resentfully after some perceived slight during an insignificant workplace meeting; she, in contrast, prays for those who killed her family members. We drive ourselves nuts in exhausting obsession over the latest cellphone, newer car, latest facial wrinkle, or next promotion; yet Beatrice seems content with what little she has. She embodies what the sage second-century Rabbi Meir taught us, "Who is truly rich? The one who is content with what he has."

Who doesn't want some of that? Maybe the high-octane, Beatrice-Emmaus-glow is too intimidating right now. But greater peace, inner freedom, contentment, and a closer walk with my God? Just tell me where to sign up.

To be sure, God is always working in our hearts, even when we don't feel it. As Beatrice put it to me, "What I believe is, that when you enter in front of the tabernacle, when you go into the church, when you receive communion, you do not know what is happening, but God is doing something in your heart."

But the effects of grace are not only impalpable mystery; rather, we are called to have our lives transformed in ways that are palpable to us personally and impactful on the world around us. Skim the gospels and find story after story of such change. Jesus enjoys a meal at the house of Zacchaeus the tax collector, who is so thoroughly transformed by the encounter that he declares, "the half of my goods I give to the poor; and if I have defrauded any one of anything, I restore it fourfold" (Luke 19:8). Elsewhere, Jesus heals a paralytic, and, like so many others whose bodies Jesus heals, the heart is transformed as well: he takes up the mat, "and went home, glorifying God" (Luke 5:25).

What was true in Jesus's time is supposed to be equally true today. That is, our church exists to facilitate transformative encounters with Jesus. Vatican II said that the church's mission is to "lead [people] to the faith, the freedom and the peace of Christ." Faith, freedom, and peace are not vague abstractions; either I feel them or I don't. Equally concrete is how Pope Benedict XVI once described the effects of drawing closer to God: "You will no longer be attached to material goods, because you will feel the joy of sharing them. You will cease to be sad with the sadness of the world, but you will feel sorrow at evil and rejoice at goodness, especially for mercy and forgiveness."

Peace, joy, inner freedom, compassion, moral strength; a felt experience of being loved and a commitment to share love with others in turn. That's our promise, and what modern man or woman would not want a piece of it? Social surveys consistently characterize ours as an anxious epoch. We long for deeper hope, peace, meaning, contentment, and a sense of belonging (and too often search for these in the wrong places). Our church's promise aligns so well with this world's expressed needs. This can be our moment.

So if millions are walking away from us because their spiritual needs are not being met, then either we're not doing our jobs, or Jesus is not doing Jesus's job (And I suspect it's not Jesus who has dropped the ball).

So how can we do better? I put that question to Beatrice: "So let me ask you one last question. It sounds to me like your own spiritual growth began during your sufferings. And, as you know, most Americans and Europeans won't endure such experiences. So I wonder what you would advise your fellow Christians about how we can grow spiritually, as you have?" She smiles at me. She tilts her head. She thinks. She responds shyly, "This is a very difficult question."

She doesn't quite know, and I don't quite know either. Is that it? My conversation with this woman has resulted in a dead end? No, worse than a dead end: it's like a vision of an alluring destination became tantalizingly clear, yet I can discover no path to get there.

But that's not quite right. There is always a path. God's grace, when we cooperate with it, will change what we believe to be right and wrong, bring inner peace, reorder our value system, enhance the way we look at creation, and transform the way we treat our neighbors and just about everything else about us. It's the encounter with God that ignites the glow.

God can "do something in your heart," as Beatrice put it, in myriad ways, but it's *God* who decides how and when that happens. Neither Moses, Beatrice, nor these Emmaus disciples, for example, predicted the transformation that God worked in their lives. So why would it be any different for the rest of us? That realization only occurred to me after I had wandered down a few blind alleys in search of *the* program to turn our church into a spiritual assembly line that would unfailingly churn out transformed Christians with "the glow."

It was a pipe dream, but more importantly, blasphemous. I was inadvertently turning myself into God, as if I (or even the church, for that matter) could program or control God's Spirit among us. And, come to think of it, how silly of me to have imagined that any one devotional path within our church will guarantee felt joy and peace to both young adults and grandparents, Dutch bankers and Kenyan farmers, daily Communicants and marginal Catholics.

Scripture assures us that the Holy Spirit "blows where it will," and who was I (or any of us) to tame this Holy Spirit by squeezing God's abundant graces into one little box of prescribed tools? In fact, this moment in church history seems to be calling us to the opposite: God has blessed us with a church that is more diverse, in every way, than ever before. Some of us are moved by praying the rosary in solitude; others are uplifted by lively Praise and Worship concerts.

## HE ASKED HIMSELF: ARE WE CHANGING THEIR LIVES?

All of which seems to suggest how we will transform our church into one where more transformation happens. Instead of implicitly dictating to God where the Holy Spirit should be active, in this devotion or activity rather than another, we will discern where God's Holy Spirit seems to be working and cooperate. And just how, one might wonder, will we figure that out? Simple: just ask.

Greg Hawkins, for example, has asked about half a million times by now. He began when an unsettling thought began gnawing at him. He was proud of the church he pastored: attendance was growing, and congregants were engaged in its ministries. Things were going fabulously.

Or were they? Here's how he recalled his quandary to me, "All we knew is that more and more people were participating in the church. We have no idea if it's changing their lives, if it's making them more loving people, more willing to lay down their lives to follow Jesus." So he did something that may seem obvious but, unfortunately, remains revolutionary in our church: he decided to get some answers.

His professional background came in handy. See, he had worked in management consulting before devoting his life to ministry, so he tapped his old network to identify professionals capable of designing a groundbreaking congregational survey. Not to ask superficial questions about worship times or parking lots, mind you, but to ask whether church members were growing spiritually and what helped them to grow.

The encouraging findings? What congregants most wanted, Greg discovered, is to draw closer to Jesus, to be challenged in their faith, and to understand scripture better. But disturbing findings also emerged. Some folks were attending church weekly, yet stalled or frustrated. They were showing up but not growing as disciples: and that, after all, is the most basic mission Jesus gave us, to make disciples.

Which gets to a basic question: what is a disciple, anyway? Someone who attends church? Who recites the creed? Who donates money every Sunday? Well, the root word of "disciple" connotes a "follower," so good disciples, logically, are followers of the Lord's prime commands: to love God with one's heart and soul and to love one's neighbor as oneself. To use our Beatrice imagery, disciples should feel at least a little bit of "the glow," that is, as time goes by, they should feel the increasing peace that comes with closeness to Jesus. And that closeness will inspire them to follow Jesus more closely by heeding his prime commands: to reach out in love and service of their neighbors.

Greg told me that he had started with a wrongheaded assumption about how discipleship happens: "Our mental model was: the more we got folks involved in church activity, the more it would make them loving people." The assumption was that, "activity in the church predicted spiritual growth, spiritual growth meaning increasing love of God and increasing love of others, the marks of a disciple."

Wait a minute. Isn't that how it *does* work? Virtually every Catholic parish probably makes the same assumption. After all, we occasionally count the number of Mass attendees, and we always count the weekly collection. If both those indicators are pointing in the right direction, we assume that the church is doing well.

Not necessarily. After crunching the survey results, the team discovered that the best predictor of growth in discipleship was neither church attendance nor consistent financial donations. Rather, discipleship heavily correlated to one's personal relationship with Jesus. That is, do you perceive Jesus as some distant figure or close to your life? Do you see Jesus merely as an admirable human role model or as your Lord God?

And the key to deepening that disciple-relationship is not much different than building a relationship with one's spouse or kids: "You need to spend time with the person," Greg said, and you need to communicate. It's not merely punching the clock at church each Sunday, Greg discovered, but "you had to do other things on your own time, like prayer, like reading scripture, and so on." As I listened, Beatrice's story popped back to mind and validated Greg's comments. Recall that the pre-conversion Beatrice "had the idea of a God who is very, very far away, someone who didn't know me or my circumstances." After her transformation, she has been moved to spend more time with God in prayer.

## MOVE TOWARD A TRANSFORMED LIFE

Greg and his colleagues called their survey *Reveal*, because it "reveals" the different stages of spiritual growth that Christians go through. If undertaken congregation-wide, the survey can reveal what percentage of congregants are growing spiritually and what proportion are stalled. They published their findings in a book called *Move*, as in: we can begin to pinpoint what helps people to "move" toward stronger commitment, deeper discipleship, and a transformed life. Or, in this chapter's shorthand, we can help move people toward "the glow." Here's how Greg summarized the overall objective: "What we were trying to find were the disproportionately catalytic things, either that the church did or that individuals could do, to bring about spiritual growth."

Many of the findings are intuitive: private time spent in prayer or scripture reading is highly catalytic of a deeper relationship with the Lord. If we want to help Catholics get the glow and grow in discipleship, we have to encourage scripture reading and a prayer life beyond what takes place in Mass on Sunday. That seems obvious, so obvious that one wonders why we don't stress its importance every Sunday in every single parish. Too many parishes are not providing sufficient encouragement and tools to help us develop a prayer life.

Another of their findings seemed hugely exciting for our revitalization project. Do you know what is one of the most powerful catalysts, an almost certain spur to spiritual growth? Service of others. "That's one of the best ways the church can support my spiritual growth," Greg said, "by encouraging me to serve, commissioning me to serve." My spirits surged at that statement, because I could almost literally hear two vital elements of our strategy click snugly together. Lousy strategies often feel like to-do lists of discrete initiatives that don't seem to relate much to each other. Conversely, in the best strategies, the initiatives are mutually reinforcing. Each one builds on and supports the others.

How encouraging, then, that the act of serving also catalyzes transformation; the more we love our neighbors, the closer we feel to Jesus. And vice versa: the more one grows spiritually, the more energized one is to love and serve, simply because one wants to follow Jesus more closely by doing what Jesus instructed. That's what strategists call a "virtuous circle": serving others helps to transform you, which makes you more desirous to serve, which further transforms you, which, well, you get the idea.

But let me reveal something about Reveal. Greg Hawkins, the pastor who initiated Reveal, is not *Father* Greg Hawkins. And when Greg Hawkins talks about worship services, he is not talking about Mass. Put plainly, he ain't one of us Catholics. He's pastored at large, nondenominational churches like Willow Creek, outside of Chicago, and Oak Hills, in Texas. A few readers may have heard of those fast-growing churches and may even know one-time fellow parishioners who now attend Willow Creek or Oak Hills. Those millions whose spiritual needs are not being met within the Catholic Church? A lot of them end up at places like Willow Creek.

## WHAT COULD BE MORE INTIMATE?

But even though Greg Hawkins is not Catholic, he understands us well. I asked if his survey findings revealed any unique lessons for us Catholics? "It's not like former Catholics are different than anyone else in our survey," he starts out. He and colleagues have diced their data by age-group, religion of birth, you name it. And no matter how they slice the survey, they still uncover the same spiritual needs: people want to grow closer to Jesus. And then comes his punch line: "If anyone should get this, it's the Catholics, because of what you believe about the Eucharist. . . . I mean: to take in the body and blood of Christ: what could be more intimate than that in terms of drawing closer to Jesus?"

What *could* be more intimate than that?

All in all, he gave me new insight into our tradition. We tend to regard people as "good Catholics" when they do the "basics," like attending Sunday Mass, and as "better" Catholics when they do extras, like the rosary or spiritual reading. Greg invites us to a different mindset. Instead of just counting bodies and activities, we should be asking how and whether the sacraments and devotions are transforming parishioners and spurring spiritual growth. If so, let's redouble efforts where God's Spirit is blessing us. If not, let's dig deeper and ask our parishioners: why not? Are the Masses irreverent or sloppy? The homilies boring? Is the parish challenging members to read scripture and pray? Is the parish offering varied prayer and devotional styles that resonate with its diverse flock? And, importantly, what about those who no longer show up: why did they stop coming and what will lead them back to us? Most fundamentally: does the parish intentionally work to promote spiritual growth and deeper discipleship, or is it a tired place that is just sort of going through the motions?

Some readers may be unconvinced by the "just ask" approach. My Irish-born mother never missed a Sunday Mass and was never surveyed about her spiritual growth, and she managed just fine, thank you very much. Well, that worked for me and my mother and the "cradle to grave" Catholics of yesteryear, but it's not working for the millions of one-time Catholics who have decamped for other Christian churches, the current Catholics who aren't spiritually engaged enough to attend Mass regularly, or the legions of young adults who find the church irrelevant. Vatican II spoke of reading "the signs of the times," and there could be no clearer sign to us than this vast number of disengaged or fallen-away Catholics. Our way of doing things as a church needs to change if we want to become more effective at our mission.

An example underscores the point. In spring of 2016, Chicago's Archdiocese conducted a "Renew My Church" survey, asking exactly the questions that we need to ask: is your parish inspiring you to be a better Catholic? Would you recommend it to others? The survey invited parishioners to pinpoint challenges: is the church welcoming enough? Are the homilies effective? Does the parish need more active lay leadership, stronger financial or pastoral management, or more effective programs for learning about the faith?

Great questions and a great process. Imagine what rich insights will emerge for Chicagoland's church. Only one problem, which illustrates how dramatically our culture of accountability has to improve. The survey was launched in 2016, about a year after a new archbishop had come into office and come to grips with the archdiocese's considerable challenges, concluding that parishes would certainly have to close. The archbishop (now a Cardinal) announced the survey against that bleak backdrop, saying that Chicago faced "tough choices and new sacrifices," so that "by the time this consultative process is complete, we will mourn together the loss of some parishes."

Well, the time for a spiritual health checkup is not once problems are already so dire that some parishes will inevitably die anyway. Rather, just as with our bodily health, parishes and dioceses need routinely scheduled spiritual checkups, in order to spot and heal festering maladies early on. What's more, such annual survey/checkups will also pinpoint areas of strength, where the Spirit has been working powerfully. We can then replicate, for example, the prayer group that works well at this parish, the young adult group at that one, or the homeless outreach ministry at a third. We will be able to see where the Holy Spirit's blessings have been raining down or, alternatively, where the church is suffering a spiritual drought and hard questions must be asked.

Fortunately, our church is catching on to this. The Catholic Leadership Institute (CLI), for example, is one of various organizations that have ventured into the "just ask the Holy Spirit" business. They have crafted the Disciple Maker Index. CLI's Matt Manion warned me that the tool is still in pilot phase, but after 60,000 Catholics in dozens of parishes have participated, some valuable findings seem to be emerging. For example, Catholics seem to be most inclined to recommend parishes that help them to grow spiritually, form them as disciples, are welcoming, and feature good preaching and an enriching Mass experience. Read that list again: how encouraging that parishioners' expressed needs correspond so well with the mission Jesus gave our church. It's not like parishioners mostly care about whether the church parking lot empties quickly. No, Jesus told us to form disciples, and what parishioners want is to become better disciples (and they will gladly recommend the parish that helps them along that journey).

What's more, how encouraging that such survey tools give the church what we strategists call "actionable intelligence." In other words, we won't have to run parishes based on hunches or personal preferences, stressing folk music because the music minister prefers it or eliminating bible study because the new pastor doesn't like it. Rather, we will be guided by facts, regularly surveying parishioners to understand what is and is not driving spiritual growth. We can celebrate and grow our successful initiatives and entrepreneurially seek to restructure unsuccessful ones.

Granted, a handful of lazy, defensive, or insecure pastoral leaders may resist the effort: *we haven't done it before; why should we bother now?* A few parish leaders won't want to ask the questions because they will fear the answers. But if pastors or parish councils are unwilling to hold themselves accountable, we rank-and-file parishioners should be courageous and accountable enough to ask why important questions are not being asked. But I bet that the local bishop beats us to it. After all, the Catechism assigns the bishop "pastoral responsibility" for his diocese: to exercise that ministry "responsibly," a bishop will surely want sound data, not just anecdotes, about his flock's spiritual health.

## GETTING THE GLOW: BECOMING A CHURCH THAT TRANSFORMS HEARTS AND SOULS

Our church is called to catalyze conversion so that all of us might become disciples who more and more "love God with our whole hearts and love our neighbors as ourselves." Unfortunately, in many millions of cases, we are falling short of fulfilling that mission of transformation. Many have left us because their spiritual needs were unmet; others remain nominally Catholic but disengaged.

But the encouraging news is that we have all the resources needed to get better outcomes. We can and will do so much better. After all, our tradition is blessed with such riches. Countless millions are already finding peace, inner freedom, and joy in the Catholic Church. Conversion and inner transformation are already happening every hour of the day, in Eucharistic Adoration, vibrant charismatic prayer circles, daily attendance at Mass, prayerful reading of scripture, during spiritual direction, in walks through the countryside, among catechists, confessors, teachers, and nurses, while visiting the dying, serving lunch to the homeless, tending a sick child, or showing compassion to one's spouse.

We want everyone who encounters our church to experience the same profound spiritual growth that so many millions are already enjoying. So, we'll become accountable enough to ask the questions that will reveal where that is happening in our parishes and our ministries. Where it is, we'll thank God and try to cooperate even more energetically with the Spirit's work. Where it's not, we'll be courageous and entrepreneurial enough to make changes.

So far, we've established "wet socks" and "the glow" as two priorities for action. That is, we will focus our energies on serving those in need and on transforming the hearts and souls of Catholics by facilitating a journey to greater peace and joy. But one critical gap remains in our strategy. We can't serve those we have never met. And we can't transform the lives of those who remain outside our doors. Thus we turn to the final building block of our strategy: we need to reach out.

## *Pray, Reflect, Discuss, and Act*

- Pray and read scripture every day. And pray every day for your own transformation into a closer follower of the Lord.

- For individuals, small groups, and parishes: What spiritual practices help me to "get the glow," that is, to grow in my spiritual life as a disciple of Jesus? What could I start doing tomorrow (and every day thereafter) that would further my growth? How could I help others around me to grow?

- For parishes and dioceses: Survey congregants annually to assess whether they are growing in discipleship. What is helping and impeding their progress: are liturgies and homilies enriching? Is the parish offering easy-to-access devotional, prayer, or reflection opportunities that appeal not just to a few but to the diverse parish community?

- For pastors: Regularly call congregants to grow closer to the Lord, including through proven practices like bible reading and personal prayer (one effective approach can be a parish-wide 10/10 challenge: that is, challenging everyone in the parish to undertake ten minutes of bible reading and ten minutes of personal prayer every day).

# CHAPTER TEN

# Dusty Shoes

## *A Church That Reaches Out to Engage the World*

WE'RE CRAFTING A STRATEGY TO REVITALIZE OUR CHURCH. FIRST, WE focused on *how* we'll do it—by instilling a new culture where everyone leads and by becoming more accountable and entrepreneurial in everything we do.

Then we moved on to *what* we'll do. We'll channel our energies toward three priorities: we'll love and serve anyone in need; we'll transform the hearts and souls of those who pray with us; and, in this chapter, we'll reach out to those who have never heard of us, have drifted away, or who feel marginalized. In shorthand: wet socks, the glow, and dusty shoes. By heeding the lessons behind those three iconic images, we'll turn our church into what it can be.

I'm sure we can succeed with those first two priorities: after all, they entail focusing more energy where we already have enormous strengths. Serving the needy? Our church is already the world's largest provider of charitable services and an outspoken advocate for a more just world. Transform lives? Every day, millions of us are being transformed by encounters with Jesus, whether with fellow parishioners at Mass, in solitary Bible study, in small prayer groups, or in countless other ways. The nineteenth-century priest and poet Gerard Manley Hopkins, S.J., had it right; truly, Christ is among us, "play[ing] in ten thousand places."

But what are our prospects for success when it comes to reaching out, this chapter's focus? My confidence momentarily deserted me. I thought of an old mantra: culture eats strategy for lunch. That is, strategies fail when they clash with an organization's deeply ingrained habits of thinking and behaving, when culture eats strategy for lunch. If an organization's new strategy calls for speedy response in a fast-paced world, for example, that strategy will fail if the organization's bureaucratic culture tends toward lots of meetings before doing anything. Culture can either fit or frustrate a strategy, be wind at the organization's back or an anchor that impedes forward momentum.

Unfortunately, the latter is the case when it comes to reaching out and engaging the world beyond our doors. We're not good at it. It was a remarkable strength twenty centuries ago, when we were an insignificant sect within Rome's great empire, and a few dozen men and women reached out to engage the Gentile world creatively.

Somewhere since then, we've lost that knack. Perhaps that's not surprising. As the Catholic Church became a dominant religious and cultural presence in country after country, we became more like gatekeepers than door-openers. We waited for families to present babies for baptism and for parents to enroll children in our schools. We took for granted that Catholics would remain practicing Catholics, generation after generation, because that's what they always did.

Except now, that's not what they do. The culture outside our church doors has changed dramatically, but our culture has changed little. Frankly put, we are in many ways better suited for success in the world of seventy years ago than in the world God has given us today. We have become expert at lamenting and critiquing the secular, individualistic, consumerist culture in which we find ourselves. Well, we're not here merely to criticize the culture; we must figure out how to thrive in this world. An old cliché seems relevant: if there is wind, some build walls; others build windmills. Our church's future is not to wall ourselves off from the world, but, metaphorically speaking, to be windmill builders, who figure out how to turn modernity's energies to our advantage.

That means changing how we think and behave. Consider, for example, our recent history of trying to launch new initiatives. John Paul II called for "new methods and expressions." He and his successor, Pope

Benedict XVI, championed a "New Evangelization." Yet, though these popes heralded the New Evangelization as the church's most important priority, toward which "all its energies" would be committed, nothing like that ever happened. Relatively few Catholics know about it, can explain it, or have taken up roles in it. No surprise, then, that this much-heralded effort has basically failed.

Culture eats strategy for lunch, and the "new evangelization" exposed our cultural weaknesses. By definition, a "new" evangelization calls for new methods and entrepreneurial spirit, yet we can point to little that is new. And we failed the good steward's first test of accountability: goals were never articulated in concrete terms; we could never really say what success would look like; and we never monitored or evaluated outcomes. And, insofar as it did go poorly, no one was in danger of losing their jobs over it.

Above all, a new evangelization entails reaching out to those who don't know us or who have lost interest, and we Catholics don't like to reach out, and it showed: the effort mostly involved church-insiders talking to other church-insiders. To use the biblical analogy, we tried to pour new wine into the old wineskins of our risk-averse, bureaucratic culture.

In short, we need to catalyze a massive culture shift, and another mantra will help us to get going: it's easier to act your way into a new way of thinking than to think your way into a new way of acting. Instead of theorizing about a New Evangelization in highly conceptual terms that resonate with so few Catholics, let's catalyze action around problems that resonate painfully with many of us: that our own beloved children have lost interest, or that our beloved parish is sparsely attended and may close, or that our neighbors find the church irrelevant or, even worse, feel marginalized. These are concrete problems that all of us grasp; our anguish about them is palpable; we are therefore motivated to help remedy this slowly encroaching crisis.

So how will we start acting our way into a needed new way of thinking? A simple image will give us a goal to shoot for, and a couple of stories will illustrate how we will begin leading the church in the right direction, starting tomorrow.

## Making Our Churches Feel Like Home

Bishop McElroy gives us an image. We met him earlier, at a retreat where young Catholics leaders opined that they found the church distant and judgmental. Fast-forward some months, and that discouraging message gives way to an encouraging one. After becoming San Diego's bishop, McElroy set out to visit every parish's priests, staff, and lay leaders. When asked to describe their respective parishes, one after another told him, "I feel like it is a home to me."

How consoling that must have been to hear. And what a great goal to shoot for: we want people to feel at home in our church. Because that's what Jesus wants. As in every other chapter, we go to Jesus as our strategic touchstone, and so much of Jesus's iconic imagery centers on welcome and homecoming: the father who is overjoyed because his prodigal son has returned home; the shepherd who searches for the lost sheep; the Father and Son who will "make their home" (John 14:23) with those who keep the Lord's word; the Lord who says, "Come to me, all who are heavy-burdened." The apostle Paul sums it up succinctly: "Welcome one another, then, just as Christ welcomed you" (Rom. 15:7).

That's Jesus's vision. But as the storied American inventor Thomas Edison once put it, "Vision without execution is hallucination." Too many of our neighbors don't feel welcome and don't see the church as their home. It does no good to preach a theoretical welcome that is never felt by those who have left the church or grown lukewarm; we need deeds that will bring Jesus's ancient vision to modern life. Fortunately, we can immediately take baby steps toward becoming a more welcoming church, and two stories will show us how.

The first dates back to my freshman year of high school, when our religion teacher assigned us to visit a Protestant service and compare it to a Catholic Mass. My first problem with that assignment? Finding a Protestant church in my Catholic and Jewish neighborhood. Plenty of churches were nearby, but only "home team" churches like St. Joan of Arc or Our Lady of Fatima. A Protestant church? I trolled through the phone book, found an A.M.E. church (whatever that meant), scribbled the address, and asked my father to drive me there.

As my father navigated toward the address in a pre-GPS era, my anxiety at attending an unfamiliar church began rising to full-on dread as the car crossed Junction Boulevard, the dividing line between (white) Jackson Heights and (black) Corona. Once we drew close, it was easy to pick out the church. Men milled outside in suits, joined by women in bright dresses and showy hats. My father pulled up out front, I read the church billboard, and I learned what A.M.E. stands for: African Methodist Episcopal. I began a lonely march up the church steps. (If I become half the man that my father was, I will be twice the man that I am today. But I still harbor a tiny nugget of childhood resentment that he hadn't taken note of my obvious discomfort, put an arm around me, and offered to accompany me.)

I sat alone in the very back pew, dying of near embarrassment. I remember nothing of the service save a sea of black faces, bright hats, and two moments. Early on, the pastor warmly welcomed newcomers to the congregation and asked that each visitor stand to be welcomed with applause. Well, 200 black worshippers were aware that a white visitor sat among them, but this thirteen-year-old kid was too shy to stand, and the pastor too kind to single him out, and the congregants too hospitable to swing around in their seats and eyeball the uptight white kid who seemed to have taken a seriously wrong turn and ended up in their exuberant midst.

But when the service ended, one woman did turn around. I remember her as ancient, though she might well have been only sixty; and I see her taking one of my hands into both of hers, though that too could be my imaginative reconstruction. But I have no doubt that I remember, almost to the word, what she said to me: "I want to tell you that when I first came to this church it was many years ago, and I sat by myself just like you did today. So if you want to come back next week, I want you to come up here and sit right next to me."

I was a frightened thirteen-year-old who just wanted to get out of there, but I could nonetheless perceive that something beautifully, vitally Christian had happened. I forget the report that I wrote for my religion class. I probably wrote that "they" didn't have Holy Eucharist at their church, but I was smart enough to perceive that they had something that we didn't, the willingness to reach out and make a stranger feel at home. I've visited hundreds of Catholic churches since, and only twice has anything like that welcome to a stranger ever happened.

## CREATING A CULTURE OF WELCOME: A LONG WAY TO GO

That episode had lain dormant in memory's recesses until Elder Walt brought it back to mind during a recent visit to Wallingford Presbyterian Church, where a friend was singing at the principal Sunday worship service. My wife and I had settled into a pew when a gentleman walked over and introduced himself. He said he hadn't noticed us before, wondered if we were visitors, and welcomed us.

Well, that was apparently routine for Presbyterian Walt, but not for Catholic Chris, so I sidled up to Walt at the coffee hour after the service. It turned out that Walt's hello was only an initial gesture in their broader culture of welcome. He showed me an index-card sized form: visitors are invited to leave contact information, the pastor personally writes each visitor, thanks them for coming, and invites them back. If they want to learn a bit more about the congregation's beliefs, the church's brochure rack features "Welcome to Wallingford Presbyterian Church," and "Learn about being a Presbyterian."

The parishes near my home do none of that. In fact, only a tiny, inconspicuous sign identifies one of them as a Catholic church; no signboard announces worship times. If they are trying to discourage visitors, they are doing a pretty good job. But not to worry: the first steps toward becoming more welcoming will be so simple and inexpensive that thousands of parishes can implement them next week, simply by complying with the ten commandments.

No, not *those* Ten Commandments, rather the ten commandments for a more welcoming church. Various online versions of that list emphasize commonsense steps, such as: the parish answering machine must have a prompt for those who want to learn more about the church; the weekly parish bulletin must include a welcome message; each parishioner must be asked periodically to invite someone to church or to a church activity; those who have stopped attending Mass must be called and welcomed back (*and* asked sincerely for any constructive feedback on the parish); parishioners must greet anyone sitting beside them in church whom they do not recognize, and so on.

Is someone really going to become Catholic because of an answering machine message? Shouldn't people be drawn instead by our substance: our history, sacraments, saints, and intellectual tradition? Well, let's ask one of our intellectual tradition's most substantial luminaries, St. Augustine, who was first drawn not by turgid rhetoric but by the friendliness of Ambrose, his mentor. As Augustine wrote: "I began to love [Ambrose] at first not as a teacher of the truth (for I had quite despaired of finding it in [the] Church) but simply as a man who was kind and generous to me."

Countless men and women stand in pagan-Augustine's shoes. They don't "despair" of finding truth in our church, because they're not even curious; we're essentially irrelevant to them. Our first step toward them is to be "kind and generous," like Ambrose; or, as Jesus put it to two curiosity seekers who later become disciples, "Come and see." Come to see us at worship, or work beside us in our soup kitchen, or sit in on our bible study or centering prayer groups. What will they see when they come? Hopefully, they will walk away feeling some of the following: I want some of what those guys got; I could find my home in this community; these guys are not the judgmental bigots I heard they were; I was uplifted; they care about the things that I most deeply care about; something uniquely true and life-giving was there.

And if they feel none of these things? Well, that will be our wake-up call to greater accountability. A close friend read this draft manuscript and remarked: "Chris, I get your point about being more welcoming, but I'd frankly be too embarrassed to invite someone to my parish Mass: it's so uninspired and the homilies are terrible." I'm sure she's not the only one to feel that way, and, up to now, Catholic culture has been: just deal with it; we don't criticize the priest; and we're not like some corporation that assesses everyone's performance. Sorry, all that must now change. Jesus called us to a mission, and good stewardship will entail honest assessment of why that mission is not going as well as it could be.

The focus, though, must remain on becoming a welcoming church, not on whether this or that initiative has immediately yielded converts.

That wrongheaded emphasis will quickly degenerate into proselytism, a manipulative effort to lure people, devoid of the profound respect for their current beliefs and freedom of conscience. Pope Francis called such proselytism, "solemn nonsense," and Pope Benedict was equally straight-forward: "the Church does not engage in proselytism."

Recall another of this book's maxims: we will succeed in the twen-ty-first century by wielding the fascinating power of love in a world that too often manifests the opposite. Apply that maxim to this chapter's theme: nothing will be fascinating about outreach that masks a thinly veiled agenda to fill pews and collection baskets. After all, every orga-nization from the Rotary Club to the Republican Party wants to swell its membership ranks. What will truly fascinate, in contrast, is friendly outreach and charity motivated primarily by human solidarity. And what will fascinate even further will be our attitude, namely, that we have something to gain from every relationship and something to learn about human experience even (perhaps especially) from those who disagree with or feel marginalized by our teachings, like our divorced brothers and sisters, those in homosexual relationships, and so on.

## The Statistic That Shames Us: Six Out/One In

A few statistics highlight how far we have to go. When Pew researchers asked those who had switched churches why they first attended their new church, fully 30 percent of them had a straightforward response: someone invited me. Not the church's theological foundations, splendid archi-tecture, or even its accessible parking. Just: someone invited me. Well, someone must be doing all the inviting, and, sure enough, 87 percent of Protestant megachurch attendees have said that they invited someone to church within the last twelve months; I'm not sure the comparable statistic even exists for us Catholics. I can only testify that I myself have never been urged from the pulpit to invite an outsider to a Mass, to sit in on a bible study, or even for a tour of the church.

We are now reaping the disastrous results of that unwelcoming spirit. An earlier chapter cited a damning finding from a recent Pew Research study. We Catholics fall abysmally short of other denominations when it comes to attracting new members. We attract only one new adherent for every six we lose; no other denomination does nearly so poorly. The researchers bluntly laid out the facts: "12.9 percent of American adults are former Catholics, while just 2 percent of US adults have converted to Catholicism from another religious tradition. No other religious group in the survey has such a lopsided ratio of losses to gains."

The initiatives noted above will be challenging enough but are merely "baby steps" toward a culture of outreach, and baby steps alone won't suffice. It won't suffice merely to welcome people at our doors, for a straightforward reason: people aren't even approaching our doors. The young adults are not, vast numbers of Europeans, Americans, Australians, and others are not, increasing numbers of Catholics-turned-Pentecostal in Africa or South America are not, those who were alienated by the church's handling of pedophilia scandals are not, not to mention those who feel marginalized by their poverty, mental illness, infirmities, illegal status, sexual identity, or in countless other ways. "These people have lost trust," Pope Francis once said, "they don't have the courage to knock on the doors of our Christian hearts, the doors of our churches."

Those who bridle indignantly at the Pope's blunt assertion can pray over an anecdote. A Catholic friend participated in an ecumenical initiative, where various denominations each took turns hosting their fellow Christians for fellowship and prayer. As the Salvation Army's turn drew near, an acquaintance had quipped to her, "I just hope your sense of smell isn't very good." True enough, her olfactory nerves were tormented as she prayed at the Salvation Army service among street people, addicts, and mentally disturbed worshippers. But her conscience as a Catholic was even more deeply tormented as she thought: why don't I see these people worshipping among us Catholics? We preach the same respect for the dignity of all persons as the Salvation Army does. The difference? The Salvation Army reaches out, while our words go unmatched by commensurate deeds.

We will go out and engage all those outside our doors, not hang back and merely say they are welcome. Once again, the twenty-first-century solution will be to rediscover first-century Jesus. Remind yourself how the prodigal son story unfolds: the son leaves with his inheritance, blows it frivolously, is reduced to menial labor, repents of his foolishness, and returns home to find his forgiving father waiting to welcome him with a party, right?

Wrong. The father doesn't *wait* for the son, but, "while [the son] was yet at a distance, his father saw him and had compassion, and ran and embraced him and kissed him" (Luke 15:20). Three details illustrate the culture we will create. First, the father saw the son, "while he was yet at a distance," that is, instead of focusing primarily on internal church affairs, we should be perennially looking outward, scanning the horizon for those "yet at a distance" from us. Second, the father "ran to greet him," that is, instead of waiting for people to find their way to us, we must "run" out to them. And, third, he "embraced and kissed him," *before* the son got the chance to utter a repentant word. The father runs out to meet him anyway, full of hope and hospitality; what an extravagant welcome for someone who has recently blown half of the family assets.

## SICKENED FROM THE STALE AIR OF CLOSED ROOMS

That same spirit surfaces continuously in Jesus's words and deeds. The good shepherd doesn't patiently wait for the lost sheep to return but goes out and searches. Jesus doesn't wait for the tax-collector Zacchaeus to amend his evil ways but reaches out, asking nothing of Zacchaeus but a little time (and a free meal at Zacchaeus's house).

One of Pope Francis's greatest legacies may be his desire to transform us into a church that reaches out like Jesus. He told bishops in Brazil that: "we need a Church capable of walking at people's side, of doing more than simply listening to them: a church which accompanies them on their journey." Early in his pontificate, he said that, "A Church that does not go out of itself, sooner or later, sickens from the stale air of closed rooms," and he warned that, "We have to become courageous Christians and seek out those who need help most." Among his most arresting images is that of the church as field hospital after a battle. Our calling is to the front lines of modern life, where people are hurting, struggling, defeated, or discouraged.

The emphasis on reaching out did not just occur to him during a slow afternoon at the Vatican; it's characterized his whole priestly life, as evident in the story that yields this chapter's icon-image, the dusty shoes. An Argentine Jesuit told me that then-Fr. Bergoglio was asked to launch a new parish in a shantytown of shacks and rutted dirt paths. Bergoglio huddled with a few seminarian helpers one evening, sketched a crude map of the neighborhood, and assigned each volunteer to cover part of the barrio.

And do what, they wondered? "Just walk the neighborhood," Bergoglio told them, "visit everyone." Don't wait for people to come to us; meet them where they live. My storyteller still remembered some of Bergoglio's slogans: "visit the poor and take care of their needs," and "get the kids for religious instruction." Later on, how did Bergoglio assess which of the volunteers were doing what needed to be done? Simple. He would hang around the seminary entrance as one volunteer after another trailed home from this outreach, and Bergoglio would glance down, noting whose shoes are dusty.

Earlier on, Bishop McElroy gave us a guiding vision for this chapter: making everyone feel at home. And Fr. Bergoglio now gives us a guiding image for how we will make that happen: we need to get our shoes dusty.

That will mean something different in every part of the world, and in every parish and ministry. Here's one example out of a million. Recall Philadelphia's Father Chris Walsh, one of the new leaders profiled in an earlier chapter. One of his great entrepreneurial strengths is knowing that he doesn't know all the answers, and he won't find them by hunkering down in his rectory office. He knows he has to get his shoes dusty, in this case literally.

Chris told me about an outreach initiative where he and a few parishioners resolved to walk their neighborhood, knock on house doors, inquire whether the parish could be of any assistance, and invite neighbors to learn more about the parish. That sounds like Bergoglio's strategy, but what works in Buenos Aires may not work in Philly. The experiment was a disaster. Most neighborhood residents didn't even open their doors to the smiling, burly white guy and his black sidekicks. Were they salespeople, con artists, or just harmless nutcases?

A disaster, but so what? One of the guiding mantras of successful entrepreneurs is "fail fast." That is, don't plan endlessly; try something, and, if the pilot seems promising, fine-tune it as you go. But if the pilot looks hopeless, then "fail fast": harvest lessons learned and move on rather than watering a dead stick. Accordingly, Chris and team abandoned their neighborhood visits and eventually hit upon an idea that is supremely elegant in its simplicity. Many non-parishioners and non-Catholics send their children to the parish primary school, highly regarded because of its values, discipline, and culture of learning. The parishioners had a brainstorm: instead of knocking on the doors of folks who don't even know us, why not spend time with those who already respect us?

So, nowadays, at the school's parent-teacher nights, a side table invites parents to learn more about the parish and its ministries. That simple idea has already attracted some new worshippers or volunteers for the parish's services to the needy. That simple initiative could be replicated in a few hundred more parish schools this year, and if it's not road tested in at least a few dozen, then shame on us for our inability to function as a high-performing network of spirited entrepreneurs who learn from each other's successes.

Of course, that particular idea can only be replicated if a parish has a school, which gets to an obstacle on the road to building our outreach culture. It's easier when you have lots of what I call "touch points," opportunities to interact with your neighbors, through Catholic grammar schools, colleges, hospitals, social service agencies, soup kitchens—you name it. Those are the places where newcomers "come and see" who we are and, hopefully, experience the same kindness and generosity that so impressed Augustine.

Pope Francis told us, "We must create a 'culture of encounter,' a culture of friendship . . . in which we can also speak with those who think differently, as well as those who hold other beliefs." Our hospitals, schools, and social service agencies are where this happens above all. Hindu, Jewish, or atheist nurses labor side by side with us in Catholic hospitals; together, we care reverently for everyone who walks through our doors, whatever their faith tradition. Together, we show the world that humans of different faith traditions can collaboratively champion shared values, like justice, charity, and the common good.

What's more, our non-Catholic collaborators, patients, students, or vendors get to see us at our best, committed to serve all and not just our fellow believers. Our early Christian ancestors fascinated the world by their indiscriminate love and service; we will do the same.

In a world that is increasingly secular and riven by religious divisiveness, these "touch points" have become invaluable, but they are becoming scarcer: thousands of Catholic schools and hospitals have closed in recent decades. Thus, the strategic imperative to find new ways to reach out and engage those outside our church doors. And not only has the declining number of institutional touch points hobbled us but also an occasional aversion to "touching" those who think differently. That is, zeal for a "purer" Catholic church can lead some of us to look askance even at fellow Catholics who do not subscribe to every iota of church teaching, or whose Catholic practice may be lax.

We should be pulling in rather than pushing away these "fringe members." That's what Christian charity would tell us, and that's what "social capital theory" would tell us too: in other words, now that our institutional presence of parishes and schools is dwindling in many neighborhoods, we need to find other ways of connecting people to us (this "connectedness" to the community, which was the genius of our parish structure in its heyday, is what academics call "social capital"). In other words, we want lots of people to know us, interact with us, and tell themselves and their neighbors: *well, I don't yet agree with everything the church teaches, but they welcome me warmly, and I sure do value and respect their lived commitment to holiness and charity; I want to be somehow connected to them.*

Let's face it: we have to build a better "culture of encounter" not only with nonbelievers, but even with our own fellow Catholics. Catholic thought leaders have been carving themselves into tribes for decades: we label each other as progressives and traditionalists, forces of rupture and forces of continuity, dissenters and believers in the spirit of Vatican II; each Catholic tribe seems to have its own favored Popes, websites, and periodicals. It's madness: precisely when we need to rally together to revive our struggling church, we're carving each other up. We're thumbing our noses at one of Christendom's most ancient prayer-hymns, the venerable *Ubi Caritas*, which warns us: "*Cessent jurgia maligna, cessent lites*" (Let all malicious wranglings and contentions cease).

And if ideology sometimes divides one Catholic from another, the disease of *my*-profession-above-*our*-mission sometimes divides one Catholic institution from another, just when we need to be more collaborative. Catholic universities, for example, network with other universities, hospitals with hospitals, and parishes with parishes. Each floats in its own specialized orbit; we rarely meet across specialties to explore shared priorities. The EASTeR project can bring us back to the same table. As Catholic institutions, we have a shared mission to serve the poor, transform hearts and souls, and reach out to the world. How can we do that together (and not just separately)? How, for example, can the Catholic hospital help the parish in our shared mission, and vice versa?

## DUSTY FEET IN CYBERSPACE

Our inability (or unwillingness) to rally around a shared strategy has hobbled our outreach to so many groups, not least our own beloved children. Research shows that fully two-thirds of all those who abandon Catholicism do so by the age of twenty-three; therefore, teens and early adults, our most vulnerable population, should be a foremost focus of our outreach and ministry. It's unconscionable, then, that we often let them disappear from our ministerial radar during these high-risk years. Look around your church and read your parish bulletin: chances are, very little that goes on will be focused toward the young, whether Mass times, worship styles, outreach activities, and so on.

Here's where a coordinated, one-team mindset could accomplish so much more than our currently fragmented approaches. Very few parishes will be able to mount a credible young adult outreach on their own, for example, but a cluster of parishes sure could, all the more so if these parish clusters partnered entrepreneurially with Catholic social service and health care ministries to imagine volunteer service opportunities that might appeal to young adults.

And our outreach efforts to the young could be utterly transformed by the potent alchemy of two drops of entrepreneurial imagination mixed with a dash of technology. Young adults are perpetual motion machines who transition from home parish in one town to university in another to jobs in yet a third; if we expect these peripatetic young adults to register themselves dutifully at new parishes after each move, then we have been smoking too much of what teenagers smoke during wayward college years. The twenty-first-century model? Each Catholic student who attends university will find a message of welcome from campus ministry: "Hey, your home parish (or Catholic high school) informed us you were coming; we would love to welcome you to campus at a reception."

A few years later, when these college graduates land jobs in a new city, they will find a similar welcome: "Hey, your university campus ministry informed us you were coming to town. Please join us at a welcome reception for new graduates. You'll meet young adult peers and mentors willing to guide the transition to work. You'll meet representatives of our homeless shelters and soup kitchens, who would love a bit of your volunteer time. You'll learn about parishes that offer young adult Masses at 9 p.m., which may suit your preference."

Such initiatives may sound administratively impossible, but only to those of us dinosaurs from the antediluvian epoch before social media. If we want to engage young adults, we are going to have to get our feet dusty, and that includes getting them dusty in cyberspace. Plenty of young adult Catholics have the skill and imagination to lead us there; we just need the willingness to empower and follow them.

But far more important than technology will be vision, solidarity, and the will to reach out. We need to see and feel ourselves as one body, no matter that age group, socioeconomic status, geographic location, or ideological predilection may superficially divide us. We Catholics say that we are members of the same family; we will now behave more like one. Some 5,000 of our family members in Nigeria's Maiduguri region, for example, have been slaughtered in recent years, found guilty of one offense only: being Christian. Very few Catholics, I suspect, have even heard of these slain family members, much less prayed for them during offertory prayers at Mass. Pope Francis has pointed out that "there are more martyrs in the Church today than in the first centuries." It says something terrible about us that these suffering and dying brothers and sisters go largely unnoticed and unmourned by us.

We Catholics will surely fascinate the outside world more thoroughly when we love each other more obviously, by showing greater solidarity with our own fellow Catholics, including those who are suffering persecution (above all) or who lack our financial resources or are not influential in the world's eyes or who happen to disagree with our theology.

## LET'S CHANGE OUR LEGACY
Six Out/One In.

How dreadful if that ends up as this Catholic generation's legacy. Yet I can think of an even worse legacy: that we didn't even try to reverse that trend, blithely brushing off the fact that virtually no other religious denomination is faring as poorly as we. An equally pitiful legacy would be that we pointed fingers at fellow Catholics instead of forging ties with them to address our challenges. But I'm confident that we won't be a generation that contented ourselves with blaming our travails on a secular culture, shrugged our shoulders, and kept doing more or less the same things in the same ways as before, embodying the cliché about insanity: doing the same thing over and over, yet expecting a different outcome.

"Dusty shoes," this chapter's strategic emphasis, is about changing that legacy by changing our culture: from an internally focused church to one that will reach out; from one that merely talks about welcome to one that will run out, like the prodigal son's father, to welcome others; from one where we Catholics bicker over our differences to one where we rally around shared priorities; from one that is well-suited for success in the world of decades ago to one that is geared for success in the world we now have.

At a synod not so many years ago, bishops issued this eloquent call: "We must form welcoming communities in which all outcasts find a home. . . . [We must] attract the disenchanted glance of contemporary humanity with the ardent force of love. . . . It is up to us today to render experiences of the Church concretely accessible, to multiply wells where thirsting men and women are invited to encounter Jesus." Yes! That's exactly it. And now is the time for deeds. What if every diocese, parish, school, hospital, and other ministry "audited" itself against that preceding excerpt? Too often, we would find that the "wells," where others can encounter us, are not "multiplying" but diminishing in number. And many "outcasts" do not "find a home" with us; rather, if they feel anything at all about us, they feel like, well, "outcasts." All that will change; we will act our way into the new way of thinking articulated at that synod.

But our outreach will succeed only when we also "reach in" to show greater love and solidarity toward our own fellow Catholics. Pope Benedict XVI correctly pointed out that the contemporary church will only really grow, "by attraction, just as Christ 'draws all to himself' by the power of his love." It does us no good to preach about love if those outside our doors don't see an attractive witness of love in action among us.

Pope Francis gets the final word on what this Christian outreach looks like at its best: "If the whole Church takes up this missionary impulse, she has to go forth to everyone without exception. But to whom should she go first? When we read the Gospel we find a clear indication: not so much our friends and wealthy neighbours, but above all the poor and the sick, those who are usually despised and overlooked, those who cannot repay you . . . there is an inseparable bond between our faith and the poor. May we never abandon them."

Amen to that.

## Pray, Reflect, Discuss, and Act

- Pray over this chapter's anecdotes: the Salvation Army story, the martyrs of Maiduguri, the author's A.M.E. church visit as a young boy. What lessons does each hold for me? Am I welcoming enough? Do I feel deep enough solidarity with fellow Catholics?

- For individuals, small groups, parishes, or dioceses: Who are we not reaching? What socioeconomic, ethnic, demographic, or other groups remain marginalized or outside our doors? Launch an immediate initiative to reach at least one of these populations; review lessons learned after six months.

- For parishes and dioceses: Within a month, develop and implement "ten commandments" for a more welcoming church—for example, that every parish will personally greet visitors, include a welcome message in each Mass and bulletin, and so on.

- For parishes and dioceses: Launch a "why have they walked away" project. Find those who have stopped attending church, politely ask why, catalogue and discuss the themes that emerge, and welcome the leavers back.

- For parishes, schools, universities, and dioceses: Launch a "No Future without the Young" project, where each region's church organizations work collaboratively on teen formation and young adult outreach programs as a crucial priority.

# CHAPTER ELEVEN

# Jolted from Tiredness

## *The Holy Spirit Has Placed Us on the Playing Field*

"WE ARE IN NEED OF BEING WOKEN FROM OUR TIREDNESS AND SHAKEN from our lack of confidence, which I believe limits the effectiveness of the church."

Archbishop Gerald Kicanas of Tucson described the church's malaise with those words a few years ago. He was speaking in the wake of horrifying sexual abuse scandals that had battered the church. But he was also mindful that millions of Catholics were becoming lukewarm or disengaged, and that these sorry trends would continue. We face a future, the archbishop said, where "the number of committed Catholics will decrease by a third."

This book's opening, the blunt assertion that we verge on crisis, was aimed at jolting us from our tiredness and complacency. I recently read a consulting firm's analysis of the "drag factors" that impede organizations from responding adequately to challenges. My stomach knotted as I noted how many of these debilitating drag factors seem to characterize our current church culture: complacency, inertia, micromanagement, and internal focus; decisions taking too long, too many organizational layers and silos, blaming others for our challenges, poor performance tolerated, groupthink, acceptance of mediocrity, taking too long to remove poor performers from key roles, and old solutions to new problems.

So, yes, while I could have told a cheery story that would make us feel warm and fuzzy, we need the opposite: an uncomfortable spur toward changing our culture and approaches so that we will accomplish more effectively the mission that Jesus gave us. We must wake up to the facts about insufficient priestly ranks, declining participation, disengaged Catholics, and worsening trends, not in the United States alone but in dozens of countries.

To pretend nothing profound is happening is either negligence or deep denial. At the same time, to pretend God's Holy Spirit is not accompanying us is blasphemous: we must pray to discern what God is saying to us through painful trends that have been worsening for decades. It's time to wake up, but not to wake up and fight (we've been doing too much of that already, fighting with each other and fighting with the world). Rather, it's time to wake up and fascinate, that is, to fascinate the world once again by the power of love.

We can succeed. Later in Archbishop Kicanas's talk, after he lamented our institutional tiredness, he noted that, "Hope looks at reality, it faces reality, it sees reality . . . yet is grounded in the realization that we live in hope, in the assurance that all will be well, that all manner of things will be well." So it is. While this writing project grounded me in the reality of our profound challenges, it more so filled me with hope. I met so many great people doing so many great things on the church's behalf. I could have written a whole chapter about how RENEW International has helped thousands of people to build communities that encounter God in everyday life; I could have written another chapter about Fe y Alegria, which helps educate nearly a million impoverished Latin Americans annually. If I tried to tell all those stories of love, goodness, charity, and reverence, well, to paraphrase John the Evangelist, the world itself could not hold all the books that would have to be written.

So, if this book's opening was a jolt from tiredness, the balance was about regaining confidence. We have everything we need to revitalize ourselves: people, beliefs, tradition, intellectual and financial resources, global reach, unity of belief, nobility of mission, and a deep sense of purpose. We don't need to become what we are not; we must only drink more deeply from our own wells by rediscovering the way in which Jesus approached persons and by embracing the early Christians' imaginative approach.

We can start making progress tomorrow. I therefore disagree with a prestigious Catholic thinker who once ventured a far bleaker prognosis. He implied that only after we hit rock bottom would we slowly begin to struggle forward: "From the crisis of today," this great theologian wrote, the church of tomorrow will emerge "a Church that has lost much. It will become small and will have to start afresh, more or less from the beginning. It will no longer be able to inhabit" and fill the buildings built in her period of splendor. It seemed "certain" to this theologian, that, "the real crisis has scarcely begun. We will have to count on terrific upheavals." The process of rebuilding the church will be "tough going," and "long and arduous," and will make the church "poor."

He was right about much: our church already has lost much. Tens of millions of one-time Catholics no longer walk with us, and many ornate churches erected during Catholic Europe's time of splendor now draw more tourists than worshippers.

## A CHURCH THAT WILL HAVE TO START FROM THE BEGINNING? NO!

The theologian who sketched this bleak vision of Catholicism's future was Rev. Joseph Ratzinger, writing in 1970. The last thing he must have then imagined was that he himself would someday preside over this church in crisis. Even though Joseph Ratzinger, Pope Benedict XVI, would speak far more insightfully about our church on his worst day than I can on my best, I take great exception to elements of that 1970 prophecy (when contradicting a Pope, better to choose an obscure, pre-Papal text). After suffering its travails, Ratzinger had written, the church will have to start over, "more or less from the beginning," and the process will be "tough going . . . long and arduous."

Sorry, I disagree. The church will be small and have to start from the beginning only if we keep pushing off an accountable appraisal of our predicament and continue to balk at imaginative responses. And the process will be long and arduous only if we continue to make it that way by refusing to acknowledge the strategies of recent decades that have simply not worked.

In fact, the work of revitalizing our church will be joyful and energizing rather than long and arduous. Let's not wait until we have lost more but start now while we still have abundant resources at our disposal. All we need is the courage to begin, and a more strategic approach to thinking through the "who, how, and what" of rebuilding our church, that is, *who* will lead the way forward, *how* will we do it, and *what* are our priorities?

## We All Must Lead

*Who will lead the way?* All of us. That's the cornerstone of our new leadership culture. No organization conquers complex challenges in a rapidly evolving world without arraying all of its talent. We are far from doing so. Our shepherds and pastors need to be much more proactive in calling and empowering Catholics to wield their gifts in every imaginable way, like Lucy's leadership of a Nairobi jumuiya, the software engineer's Preach Back app, the finance executive's cost-management ideas, Katharina's Nightfever project, or countless other ways. A leadership responsibility is inherent in the baptismal promise, and we all show leadership, for starters, by more intentionally role modeling the way of Jesus and influencing our own families and parishes to serve those in need and to reach out more effectively.

All of us must step up and lead: it's the most crucial element of our whole revitalization strategy. Granted, some of this book's suggestions contemplated parish-wide or even national initiatives. But this book's worst outcome would be for a reader to conclude: *well, I can't do much; we need the bishops and Pope to step in and do something.* No. The rest of us need to step in and do something, or else the sorry trends highlighted earlier will continue and worsen.

Remember Sr. Rita Scully, the "wet socks" sister who conceived a new ministry after hearing about dirty socks rinsed in a holy water font? Her instinctive reaction was not: *someone ought to do something about this,* but, *there's something I can do.* The church needs all of us to think that way right now. I would invite each reader, for example, whether an individual layperson or a parish priest, to pray over the five pillars of the EASTeR project and resolve, as Sr. Rita did: *here's one thing I myself can start doing tomorrow*, or *here's one thing my family could take on as a project*, or *here's one thing that I could change or influence in my parish*. If we can ignite that sort of bottom-up leadership on a global basis, then we succeed as church in this century; I'm convinced.

But beyond this, we also need top-down leadership, of course, which will further magnify the impact of our new culture where "everyone leads." For example, those in authority need to imagine how to tap more effectively the administrative, managerial, decision-making, and strategic skills of their talented lay sisters and brothers. Those in authority can flex their imagination by creating more space and better opportunities for all this talent to blossom. As Fr. Ratzinger put it elsewhere in that same text, the church that wants to revitalize itself will have to count "on the initiative of its individual members" and use their gifts by "discover[ing] new forms of ministry."

Consider one mind-stretching example: the Vatican Secretary of State is one of the church's highest-ranking offices, sometimes compared to the role of a national prime minister. The incumbent, Cardinal Pietro Parolin, told reporters that he could imagine a woman assuming his lofty role, "in the sense that the role of the Secretary of State is evidently not bound to the sacraments or the priesthood." He continued: "let's look at the path that has been traveled, and the Lord will tell us how far we can go."

If the Vatican Secretary of State can imagine a woman playing his role, how many other possibilities might emerge if we all think expansively? This has nothing to do with political correctness or tokenism and everything to do with arraying all our talent against all our weighty challenges. Legendary stock market investor Warren Buffett once wittily attributed his relative success to the advantage of competing against only half the world (that is, Buffett's field is so male-dominated that he rarely had to compete against half the planet's smartest, most resourceful citizens: women). Well, by analogy, if we are to be good stewards, we need to assure the Lord that we have used all the talent that God placed at our disposal, in every creative way we could imagine.

## TOWARD AN ACCOUNTABLE, ENTREPRENEURIAL CHURCH

*How will we lead the way forward?* By being more entrepreneurial and more accountable in every single thing we do. A more entrepreneurial church will heed Pope Francis's exhortation to "abandon the complacent attitude that says: 'We have always done it this way.'" Instead, as he put it, we must become "bold and creative in this task of rethinking the goals, structures, style and methods" of outreach. That translates into unleashing and supporting our holy entrepreneurs.

A spirit of accountability will inspire us to ask different questions, whether in parish councils, chancery offices, as trustees of charitable ministries, or in informal discussions after Mass: Can we demonstrate that we really are forming disciples who are growing closer to Jesus? Can we demonstrate that the poor really are "at the head of the line" in our parishes, diocesan budgets, and consciousness? Are we managing our human resources and financial affairs as good stewards should, that is, with uncompromising standards of professionalism and excellence that befit a vast global institution with so important a mission? By asking and answering such questions, we will assure each other (and the Lord) of good stewardship.

## WET SOCKS, THE GLOW, AND DUSTY SHOES

*What are our priorities?* Our new culture, highly entrepreneurial and energized by widely distributed leadership, will be a recipe either for revitalization or for chaos. The difference between the two outcomes lies in unity around beliefs and values and in shared priorities for action. We've articulated those priorities, each with its icon: wet socks, the glow, and dusty shoes. That is, we will serve all those in need, transform the hearts and souls of our adherents, and reach out to the world beyond our doors.

We will tap the power of a billion people who will wake up each morning with a clear sense of mission and the invigorating knowledge that millions of fellow Catholics stand shoulder-to-shoulder with them. Previously unimagined collaborative possibilities will begin to emerge as parish council members, soup kitchen managers, young adult ministers, and hospital administrators start sitting around the same table and say: I thought we were in different "businesses," but now I see that we are doing the same three things: how can we help each other? What's more, by embracing shared priorities, we will finally bury the internecine squabbles that have vitiated our church; we'll instead honor Pope John XXIII's elegant vision: in essentials, unity; in doubtful matters, liberty; in all things, charity.

Dr. Michael Brescia shows the power of our three priorities in action. He's medical director of a Catholic hospital that specializes in palliative care for the dying. Many of his terminally ill patients and their families are poor; many are not Catholic; some have never encountered the Catholic Church before this poignant moment at life's end. Dr. Brescia and his hospital are the face of Catholicism to these people. A deeply religious man, Dr. Brescia once revealed in an interview that he says a silent prayer each time he enters a patient's room.

In him, our strategy comes full circle, or, more accurately, reveals itself as a virtuous circle. When Dr. Brescia tends an impoverished, terminally ill patient and gathered family members, is that a moment of service? Or a moment where his own heart is being further transformed? Or a moment where he is reaching out to engage the world? Is it wet socks, the glow, or dusty shoes? The answer is "yes." All three things happen in that graced moment. Call our strategy "Trinity-like" in that sense: it's three-in-one.

Yes, we can and should make distinctions that will help us understand and articulate priorities as we revitalize our church. But once we've "got it," they won't feel like three distinct priorities any longer. Rather, as psychologists would put it, we'll be in the "flow," so immersed in our graced work that energy, focus, and joy are unleashed. We'll become living icons of the words that opened Pope Francis's first major pronouncement: "The joy of the gospel fills the hearts and lives of all who encounter Jesus." Ardent disciples will not talk about these initiatives as "undertaking three priorities in order to revitalize the church." Instead, they will simply say, "I'm a Christian. I'm following Jesus."

## EASTER STRATEGY FOR GOD'S EASTER PEOPLE

And so it is. We finally come to the one word that had been missing in this closing chapter, and it's the indispensable Word: Jesus. No Catholic strategy makes sense if not rooted in Jesus, and our strategy leads nowhere if not to an encounter with the Lord. Accordingly, Jesus has been the North Star to whom our strategy has been oriented. Because we are the Lord's Easter people, we pursue an EASTeR project to become more *E*ntrepreneurial and *A*ccountable as we *S*erve, *T*ransform, and *R*each out to the world. That Easter acronym is metaphorically fitting. As G. K. Chesterton quipped, "Christianity has died many times and risen again; for it had a God who knew the way out of the grave."

So it is for our church: we will rise from our current travails to new Easter life. But faith alone will not get us there. We need to think and act strategically. The world has become too complex and fast-changing for a global church to "wing it" without a focused approach to our vision. The Holy Spirit can wing it; we can't. God's every instinct is divine and unerring; ours, not quite. God is always at work in the world, but we have to work too.

And while Jesus's values and the mission he gave us are our strategy's unchanging core, the way we pursue that mission must change considerably. Vatican II spoke of reading "the signs of the times," and the signs are abundant that our current approaches are not working. As Pope Francis once put it, "we cannot simply wait for what we are experiencing to pass, under the illusion that things will return to being how they were before."

The dynamic tension between what must change and what never can is the church's drama in every era, but painfully so in our own. Many of our bishop-shepherds may feel this dilemma weighing on their collective shoulders as a great burden, and understandably so. We want to honor the church's 2,000-year-old tradition and not lead her astray. Every initiative entails risk of failure. No initiative comes with a guarantee of success. What if our strategic choices fail and leave us worse off than we already are? Well, Rabbi Noah Weinberg offers us wise counsel in this predicament, "People often avoid making decisions out of fear of making a mistake. Actually the failure to make decisions is one of life's biggest mistakes."

He's right of course. Accountable leaders in challenged organizations must gather the facts, face them, and ask themselves a simple question: if I change nothing, do I honestly think that our institution will be better off in fifteen years than it is today? Facing that question squarely is the burden (yet also the privilege) borne by leaders, whatever their field or epoch in history. Our current moment is fraught, yes, but equally pregnant with great promise. As the respected management thinker Peter Drucker once said, "We are entering a period of turbulence, a period of rapid innovation . . . but a time of turbulence is also one of great opportunity for those who can understand, accept and exploit the new realities. It is, above all, a time of opportunity for leadership."

Drucker is right. But we Christians don't primarily construe ourselves as merely leading an institution through turbulence. Rather, we are living the calling embedded in the baptismal promise. We are the ones that the Holy Spirit has put on the playing field at this moment of history. We might wish there were lots more priestly vocations, or that the culture around us were not so secular and individualistic, or that the decisions were easier, or that the church would move faster, or not have changed as much as it has, or that fellow Catholics were less obstreperous and saw things as we do.

But none of that matters right now. What matters is that we are the ones who are here, and we are here together, and God's Holy Spirit is here with us. We are the ones who are blessed and privileged with the mighty purpose of revitalizing our church.

And we will surely succeed.

# Acknowledgments

This book is immeasurably better thanks to those who freely shared their wisdom in various ways, and I'm deeply grateful to all of them. I'm indebted to those who shared their stories or insights: Matt Bannick, "Beatrice," Petra Dankova, Sal Giambanco, Fred Gluck, Sr. Marlita Henseler, Peter Karanja, Thane Kreiner, Lucy Kungu, Katharina (Fassler) Maloney, Matt Manion, Bishop James McElroy, "Monica," Pascal Mwijage, S.J., Jacqueline Novogratz, Kerry Robinson, Sr. Simone Rollman, CSR, Michael Rowan, Sr. Rita Scully, Rev. Thomas Sweetser, S.J., Fr. Emmanuel Taylor, O.P., Rev. Chris Walsh, Samuel Waweru. None of them had the chance to read or "sign off on" the manuscript, and I thank them for their generosity of spirit in contributing to a work whose ideas about the church may or may not align with their own.

Others plowed through a wordy rough draft of this manuscript and offered helpful comments. Leo Clarke, Rev. Joe Costantino, S.J., Mike Devlin, Bob Dixon, Louis Kim, Angelika Mendes-Lowney, Sr, Pat Smith, O.S.F., Christian Talbot, and Ferdinand Tablan. Rev. Agbonkhianmeghe Orobator, S.J., suggested helpful sources of input. Stefan Cornibert of Pew Research helped with research questions, as did an early meeting with Mary Gautier of the Center for Applied Research in the Apostolate. Corbinian Kyara, S.J., shared thoughts and also helped me to interview sources in Nairobi.

My wife Angelika was a patient and supportive believer in this project from the start, and her influence helped turn this book onto a better course than the one in which it was first heading. What's more, she carefully proofread the text and helped with interview translations. I'm grateful for her love. And I congratulate my nephew, Colin, on beginning his high school life so successfully.

I'm grateful to my editor, Sarah Stanton, who believed in this project and was a valued partner throughout. Her Rowman & Littlefield colleagues, including Alden Perkins, likewise brought their expertise and professionalism to every phase of the publishing process. Tabitha Carver-Roberts was a great copyeditor. Jim Fitzgerald helped with negotiating the contract.

All of these people made this book immeasurably better than it would have been otherwise. I alone am accountable for the book's many inadequacies.

# NOTES

## Chapter 1: Our Mighty Purpose: Creating the Twenty-First-Century Church

1 *a mighty one*: George Bernard Shaw, in the Epistle Dedicatory to Arthur Bingham Walkley for *Man and Superman: A Comedy and a Philosophy*, Intro Lewis Casson (New York: The Heritage Press, 1962), xxv.

2 *tens of millions*: Is it hyperbole to claim that "tens of millions" have deserted Catholicism? No; it's gross understatement. Pew research estimates that some 12.9 percent of Americans consider themselves "former" Catholics. That translates to some forty million who have deserted Catholicism *in the United States alone*. Add in large numbers of former Catholics in Brazil, Germany, France, and multiple other countries, and the real number might turn out to be a hundred million or more. For the United States, see "America's Changing Religious Landscape," *Pew Research Center: Religion and Public Life*, accessed August 2, 2016, http://www.pewforum .org/2015/05/12/americas-changing-religious-landscape/.

3 *tripling in the last few decades*: In 1980, there were 58.6 million Catholics in Africa; by 2012, that number had risen to 198.6 million. See *Global Catholicism: Trends & Forecasts* (Washington, DC: Center for Applied Research in the Apostolate, June 4, 2015), 1.

3 *priest-per-Catholic ratios are drastically worse*: Ibid., 12, 28.

3 *Latin America has been dropping for decades*: "Online Data Analysis," database for Brazil for 1995 and 2015, *Latinobarometro*, accessed August 2, 2016, http://www .latinobarometro.org/latOnline.jsp.

4 *courageous answer to this question*: Paul VI, *Evangelii Nuntiandi*, December 8, 1975, #5, accessed August 2, 2016, http://w2.vatican.va/content/paul-vi/en/apost_exhor tations/documents/hf_p-vi_exh_19751208_evangelii-nuntiandi.html.

4 *sensed an urgent duty*: John Paul II, *Redemptoris Missio* (On the Permanent Validity of the Church's Missionary Mandate), December 7, 1990, #1, accessed August 2, 2016, http://w2.vatican.va/content/john-paul-ii/en/encyclicals/documents/hf_jp-ii _enc_07121990_redemptoris-missio.html.

4 *ardor, methods, and expression*: John Paul II, *Opening Address of the Nineteenth General Assembly of CELAM* (Port-au-Prince, Haiti), March 9, 1983, *L'Osservatore Romano* English Edition 16/80 (April 18, 1983), no. 9.

4 *done it this way*: This and other quotes in this paragraph from: Francis, *Evangelii Gaudium* (On the Proclamation of the Gospel in Today's World), Nov 24, 2013, #33, #31, accessed August 2, 2016, http://w2.vatican.va/content/francesco/en/

apost_exhortations/documents/papa-francesco_esortazione-ap_20131124_evan
gelii-gaudium.html.

4 *poorly managed*: Cardinal George Pell, quoted in Gaia Pianigiani, "Vatican Finds
Stash of Money 'Tucked Away,'" *New York Times*, Dec. 4, 2014, accessed Aug. 4,
2016, http://www.nytimes.com/2014/12/05/world/europe/vatican-finds-hundreds
-of-millions-of-euros-tucked-away.html?_r=1.

### Chapter 2: Our Worst Crisis in Five Centuries?

12 *barely 5,000 remain*: "Frequently Requested Church Statistics," *Center for Applied
Research in the Apostolate*, accessed August 2, 2016, http://cara.georgetown.edu/
caraservices/requestedchurchstats.html.

13 *former times were better:* This and all subsequent scripture citations from: *The Holy
Bible* (Cleveland: World Publishing Co., 1962), Print. Rev. Standard Version.

14 *mission has taken on new forms*: Benedict XVI, *Ubicumque et Semper* (Establishing
the Pontifical Council for the New Evangelization), Sept 21, 2010, accessed August
2, 2016, http://w2.vatican.va/content/benedict-xvi/en/apost_letters/documents/
hf_ben-xvi_apl_20100921_ubicumque-et-semper.html.

15 *sickly at home*: All quotes from Sr. Marlita from e-mail correspondence with the
author in July 2015.

16 *25 percent fewer active diocesan priests:* Mark Gray, "Facing a Future with Fewer
Catholic Priests," *OSV Newsweekly*, June 6, 2010, accessed August 2, 2016, https://
www.osv.com/OSVNewsweekly/InFocus/Article/TabId/721/ArtMID/13629/Arti
cleID/4248/Facing-a-future-with-fewer-Catholic-priests.aspx. Gray's article was
written in 2010, I interpolated the percentage decrease of 25 percent, drawing on
the more current data at "Frequently Requested Church Statistics."

17 *three times a year*: Christa Pongratz-Lippitt, "Pope Says Married Men Could Be
Ordained—If World's Bishops Agree," *The Tablet*, April 10, 2014, accessed August
2, 2016, http://www.thetablet.co.uk/news/659/0/pope-says-married-men-could-be
-ordained-priests-if-world-s-bishops-agree-on-it-.

17 *minimum possible correlation*: Philip Jenkins, *The Next Christendom: The Coming of
Global Christianity* (Oxford: Oxford University Press, 2011), 3rd Ed., 203.

17 *more than three decades*: "Global Catholicism: Trends and Forecasts," 8, estimates
460.4 million Catholics in Africa by 2040. A total of 261,293 African priests would
be needed for a priest-per-Catholic ratio of 1:1,762, the current US figure. Such
growth would imply a 7 percent per annum growth rate in the number of African
priests for the next quarter century, which seems a wildly improbable outcome: in
only one year during the last decade, for example, has the number of African priests
increased by even 3.5 percent.

17 *source and summit*: *Catechism of the Catholic Church* (New York: Doubleday, 1995),
#1324. Hereafter: *Catechism*.

18 *sacramental emergency*: Megan Cornwell, "Cardinal Parolin: Scrapping Celibacy
Is No Solution to Vocations Crisis," *Catholic News Service*, Feb. 9, 2016, accessed
August 2, 2016, http://www.thetablet.co.uk/news/3036/0/cardinal-parolin-scrap
ping-celibacy-is-no-solution-to-vocations-crisis.

18 *with special difficulties*: Code of Canon Law, (Libreria Editrice Vaticana: 1983), Book II, Part II, Section II, Title III, Chapter 6, #529, accessed August 2, 2016, http://www.vatican.va/archive/ENG1104/__P1U.HTM. Hereafter: CIC (for Codex Iuris Canonici).

19 *Brooklyn and Queens*: Nicolas DiMarzio, "The Future Is Evangelization," *The Tablet*, March 8, 2008, 4.

19 *we're in big trouble*: Timothy M. Dolan, "2011: A Year for the Mass," *Catholic New York*, Dec 2, 2010, accessed August 2, 2016, http://cny.org/stories/2011-A-Year-for-the-Mass,4237?content_source=&category_id=44&search_filter=&event_mode=&event_ts_from=&list_type=&order_by=&order_sort=&content_class=&sub_type=stories&town_id.

19 *essentially no shortage*: D. Paul Sullins, "Empty Pews and Empty Altars: A Reconsideration of the Catholic Priest Shortage," Revised Aug. 10, 2000, accessed August 2, 2016, http://catholicsocialscientists.org/cssr/Archival/2001/Sullins_253-270.pdf.

20 *absence of a clergy crisis*: Ibid., 17.

20 *declining almost everywhere*: Cindy Wooden, "Statistically Speaking: Vatican Numbers Hint at Fading Faith Practice," *National Catholic Reporter*, Aug 17, 2012, accessed August 2, 2016, http://ncronline.org/news/vatican/statistically-speaking-vatican-numbers-hint-fading-faith-practice.

20 *new generations*: Ibid.

21 *dropped all the way to 60 percent*: "Religion in Latin America: Widespread Change in a Historically Catholic Country," Pew Research Center, Nov 13, 2014, accessed August 2, 2016, http://www.pewforum.org/2014/11/13/religion-in-latin-america/.

21 *Europe, previously the heartland*: Cardinal Franz König, "The Pull of God in a Godless Age," *The Tablet*, Sept 18, 1999, 4.

21 For *France*: "During Benedict's Papacy, Religious Observance among Catholics in Europe Remained Low but Stable," *Pew Research*, March 5, 2013, accessed August 3, 2016, http://www.pewforum.org/2013/03/05/during-benedicts-papacy-religious-observance-among-catholics-in-europe-remained-low-but-stable/#mass-attendance-stable-or-declining. For *Spain*: Suzanne Daley, "Catholic Clergy Protest Pope's Visit, And Its Price Tag," *New York Times*, Aug. 15, 2011, accessed August 3, 2016, http://www.nytimes.com/2011/08/16/world/europe/16madrid.html?_r=0. For *Germany*: Anian Christoph Wimmer, "German Bishops Release New Figures: Fewer Churchgoers, Parishes, and Priests," *Catholic News Agency*, accessed August 3, 2016, http://www.catholicnewsagency.com/news/german-bishops-release-new-figures-fewer-churchgoers-parishes-and-priests-63755/.

21 *by attraction*: Benedict XVI, "Church Grows by Attraction, Not Proselytism, Pope Says," *Catholic News Agency*, May 13, 2007, accessed August 2, 2016, http://www.catholicnewsagency.com/news/church_grows_by_attraction_not_proselytism_pope_says/.

21 *evangelical churches are thriving*: "Religious Switching and Intermarriage." America's Changing Religious Landscape. *Pew Research*, May 12, 2015, accessed August 2,

2016, http://www.pewforum.org/2015/05/12/chapter-2-religious-switching
-and-intermarriage/.

22  *50 percent loss through attrition*: Christian Smith, "The Situation with US Catholic
Youth Actually Is Grim," *National Catholic Reporter*, June 13, 2015, accessed August
3, 2016, https://www.ncronline.org/news/faith-parish/situation-us-catholic-youth
-actually-grim.

22  *only 7 percent . . . practicing*: Christian Smith, Kyle Longest, Jonathan Hill, and Kari
Christoffersen, *Young Catholic America: Emerging Adults In, Out of, and Gone from
the Church* (Oxford: Oxford University Press, 2014), 32–33.

22  *forty million more Hispanics*: Anna Brown, "The U.S. Hispanic Population Has
Increased Sixfold Since 1970," *Pew Research Center*, Feb. 26, 2014, accessed August
2, 2016, http://www.pewresearch.org/fact-tank/2014/02/26/the-u-s-hispanic-popu
lation-has-increased-sixfold-since-1970/.

22  *contracting dramatically*: John L. Allen, Jr., "In America's Religious Marketplace,
the Real Catholic Problem Is New Sales," *National Catholic Reporter*, Feb 11, 2011,
accessed August 2, 2016, http://ncronline.org/blogs/all-things-catholic/americas
-religious-marketplace-real-catholic-problem-new-sales.

22  *Nearly a quarter of adult Latinos*: Cary Funk and Jessica Martínez, "Fewer Hispanics Are Catholic, so How Can More Catholics be Hispanic?" *Pew Research Center*:
Fact Tank, May 7, 2014, accessed August 2, 2016, http://www.pewresearch.org/
fact-tank/2014/05/07/fewer-hispanics-are-catholic-so-how-can-more-catholics
-be-hispanic/.

23  *by 238 percent*: "Global Catholicism: Trends & Forecasts," 1, accessed July 25, 2016,
http://cara.georgetown.edu/staff/webpages/Global%20Catholicism%20Release.pdf.

23  *number of parishes has doubled*: Ibid., 25, 27.

23  *different to survive*: Martha Lagace, "Gerstner: Changing Culture at IBM—Lou
Gerstner Discusses Changing the Culture at IBM," *Harvard Business School*: Working Knowledge for Business Leaders, December 9, 2002, accessed August 2, 2016,
http://hbswk.hbs.edu/archive/3209.html.

24  *speed up the collapse*: Russell Shaw, *American Church: The Remarkable Rise, Meteoric
Fall, and Uncertain Future of Catholicism in America* (San Francisco: Ignatius Press,
2013), 190.

24  *urban Warsaw*: "Poland, Bastion of Religion, Sees Rise in Secularism," Michael
Slackman, Dec 11, 2010, *New York Times*, accessed August 2, 2016, http://www
.nytimes.com/2010/12/12/world/europe/12poland.html.

24  *Vocations . . . plummeted*: Ibid.

24  *religion is evaporating*: Ibid.

25  *Mourão, and others*: See, for example, Paulo Reis Mourão, "Determinants of the
Number of Catholic Priests to Catholics in Europe—An Economic Explanation,"
*Review of Religious Research*, Vol 52, #4, June 2011, 427–38. Also: Robert J. Barro
and Rachel M. McCleary, "Religion and Political Economy in an International
Panel," *National Bureau of Economic Research*, Working Paper 8931, May 2002.

25 *continent's high birthrate*: "Global Catholicism: Trends & Forecasts," 3: "strong growth in the number of Catholics in Africa relative to in Europe is more a phenomenon of differential fertility than immigration or evangelization."

26 *humble and courageous answer*: Evangelii Nuntiandi, #3–5.

26 *gradually stagnates*: Evangelii Gaudium, #129.

**Chapter 3: Everyone Leads: Imagining the Church's New Culture of Leadership**

30 *Example is not the main*: Erica Anderson, Ed. *Albert Schweitzer: Thoughts for Our Times* (Mount Vernon, NY: The Peter Pauper Press, 1975).

32 *follow the Pastors*: Pius X, *Vehementer Nos* (On the French Law of Separation), Feb. 11, 1906, # 6, accessed August 2, 2016, http://w2.vatican.va/content/pius-x/en/encyclicals/documents/hf_p-x_enc_11021906_vehementer-nos.html.

33 *royal mission*: Catechism, #1268.

33 *recognized as "co-responsible"*: Benedict XVI, "Opening of the Pastoral Convention of the Diocese of Rome on the Theme: 'Church Membership and Pastoral Co-Responsibility' Address of His Holiness Benedict XVI," May 26, 2009, accessed August 2, 2016, https://w2.vatican.va/content/benedict-xvi/en/speeches/2009/may/documents/hf_ben-xvi_spe_20090526_convegno-diocesi-rm.html.

33 *better structures of participation*: John Paul II, "Address of John Paul II to the Bishops of the Ecclesiastical Region of Pennsylvania and New Jersey (U.S.A.) on their 'Ad Limina' Visit," Sept 11, 2004 , #3, accessed August 2, 2016, http://w2.vatican.va/content/john-paul-ii/en/speeches/2004/september/documents/hf_jp-ii_spe_20040911_ad-limina-usa.html.

33 *strike out on new paths*: Evangelii Gaudium, #31.

35 *with special difficulties*: CIC, Book II, Part II, Section II, Title III, Chapter 6, #529.

35 *recognize and promote*: CIC, Bk II, Pt II, Sec II, Title II, Ch. 6, Can. 537, #2.

36 *share the Word*: all quotes in this discussion from discussion with the author on October 28, 2015.

38 *clericalism . . . sinful attitude*: Francis George, OMI "Developing Lay Ecclesial Ministry," in William J. Cahoy, Ed. *In the Name of the Church: Vocation and Authorization of Lay Ecclesial Ministry* (Collegeville, MN: Liturgical Press, 2012), 142.

39 *minority within the minority*: All quotes from Chris Walsh are from discussion with the author on November 29, 2015.

40 *Same Call, Different Men*: Mary L. Gautier, Paul M. Perl, Stephen J. Fichter, *Same Call, Different Men* (Collegeville, MN: Liturgical Press, 2012).

41 *only 65 percent of younger priests*: Ibid., 87.

43 *leaders of leaders*: Tim Keller, "Lay Leadership and Redeemer's Future," *Redeemer Report*, February 2010.

43 *1,000 volunteers*: Scott Thumma, "Exploring the Megachurch Phenomena: Their Characteristics and Cultural Context," *Hartford Institute for Religion Research*, accessed August 2, 2016, http://hirr.hartsem.edu/bookshelf/thumma_article2.html.

44 *higher the calling*: Adam Bryant, "Planes, Cars, and Cathedrals," *New York Times*, Sept 5, 2009, accessed August 2, 2016, http://www.nytimes.com/2009/09/06/business/06corner.html.

### Chapter 4: Follow the Leaders: Rediscovering Jesus and the Early Christians

47  *don't see the moon*: Alexander Stille, "Holy Orders: A Determined Pope Francis Moves to Reform a Recalcitrant Curia," *New Yorker*, Sep. 14, 2015, accessed August 2, 2016, http://www.newyorker.com/magazine/2015/09/14/holy-orders-letter-from-the-vatican-alexander-stille.

48  *programme for all times*: John Paul II, *Novo Millennio Ineunte* (To the Bishops, Clergy, and Faithful at the Close of the Great Jubilee of the Year 2000), Jan 6, 2001, #29, accessed August 2, 2016, https://w2.vatican.va/content/john-paul-ii/en/apost_let ters/2001/documents/hf_jp-ii_apl_20010106_novo-millennio-ineunte.html.

49  *render the Lord present*: "Synodus Episcoporum Bulletin XIII: Ordinary General Assembly of the Synod of Bishops 7-28 October 2012," Oct 26, 2012, #3, accessed Aug. 4, 2016, http://www.vatican.va/roman_curia/synod/documents/rc_synod _doc_20121026_message-synod_en.html.

49  *rediscover the ways*: Ibid., #4.

51  *would be no Heathen:* St. John Chrysostom, "Homily 10 on First Timothy," trans and ed. Philip Schaff, *Nicene and Post-Nicene Fathers*, Vol. 13 (Buffalo, NY: Christian Literature Publishing Co., 1889), edited for NewAdvent.org by Kevin Knight, accessed August 2, 2016, http://www.newadvent.org/fathers/230610.htm.

52  *favored sons and daughters*: "Thank You, Cardinal George," *Extension* (Winter 2014), 4.

59  *accounts of the Mass*: Justin Martyr: "The First Apology of Justin Martyr," Ch. 65–67. In *Writings of Saint Justin Martyr*, Thomas B. Falls, ed. (New York: Christian Heritage, Inc., 1948).

61  *stimulate progress*: James C. Collins and Jerry I Porras, *Built to Last: Successful Habits of Visionary Companies* (New York: Harper Business: 1994), 3rd edition.

### Chapter 5: The EASTeR Project: A Strategy That Can Revitalize our Church

65  *good at Plan B*: Tina Amirkiai, "Chaos Theory Shows the Wisdom of Plan B," *Chicago Council on Science and Technology*, Jan. 15, 2010, accessed August 2, 2016, http://www.c2st.org/news/2010/01/chaos-theory-shows-wisdom-plan-b-tina-amirkiai.

67  *the faith, freedom*: Second Vatican Council, "Decree *Ad Gentes* on the Mission Activity of the Church," Dec. 7, 1965, #5, accessed August 2, 2016, http://www.vatican .va/archive/hist_councils/ii_vatican_council/documents/vat-ii_decree_19651207 _ad-gentes_en.html.

68  *"business as usual" attitude*: "Synod of Bishops, XIII Ordinary General Assembly, The New Evangelization for the Transmission of the Christian Faith, Lineamenta," Feb 2, 2011, #10, accessed August 2, 2016, http://www.vatican.va/roman_curia/ synod/documents/rc_synod_doc_20110202_lineamenta-xiii-assembly_en.html.

68  *invent new strategies*: "Synodus Episcoporum XIII Ordinary General Assembly of the Synod of Bishops 7–28 October 2012 Message," #4, accessed August 2, 2016, http://www.vatican.va/roman_curia/synod/documents/rc_synod_doc_20121026_ message-synod_en.html.

69  *commit all of the church's energies*: Redemptoris Missio, #3.

69  *what his intention is*: Laurie Goodstein, "U.S. Bishops Struggle to Follow Lead of Francis," *New York Times*, Nov 11, 2014, accessed August 2, 2016, http://www

.nytimes.com/2014/11/12/us/change-urged-by-pope-francis-is-rattling-hierarchy
-of-roman-catholic-church.html.

72 *charity (diakonia):* Benedict XVI, "On the Service of Charity," Nov 11, 2012, Intro-
duction, accessed August 2, 2016, http://w2.vatican.va/content/benedict-xvi/en/
motu_proprio/documents/hf_ben-xvi_motu-proprio_20121111_caritas.html.

73 *preferential love:* Catechism, #2448.

74 *fascinating power of love:* John Paul II, "Apostolic Journey of His Holiness John Paul
II to Spain, Meeting with Young People, Address of John Paul II May 3, 2003," #3,
accessed Aug 2, 2016, http://w2.vatican.va/content/john-paul-ii/en/speeches/2003/
may/documents/hf_jp-ii_spe_20030503_youth-madrid.html.

75 *71 percent of former Catholics:* "Faith in Flux," *Pew Research Center,* April 27, 2009
(revised Feb. 2011), accessed Aug 2, 2016, http://www.pewforum.org/2009/04/27/
faith-in-flux/.

75 *stale air of closed rooms:* Francis, "Pope: Mission, the Best Cure for the
Church," April 18, 2013, accessed August 2, 2016, http://en.radiovaticana.va/
storico/2013/04/18/pope_mission,_the_best_cure_for_the_church/en1-683985.

75 *87 percent of Evangelical Christians:* Scott Thumma and Warren Bird, "Not Who
You Think They Are: A Profile of the People Who Attend America's Mega-
churches," *Hartford Institute for Religion Research,* June 9, 2009, accessed August 2,
2016, http://hirr.hartsem.edu/megachurch/megachurch_attender_report.htm.

### Chapter 6: The Catholic Elephant Can Dance: An Entrepreneurial Church

79 *energized people:* Quotes from Fr. Emmanuel from discussion with the author on
December 11, 2015.

84 *emphasis . . . on preserving things:* Quotes from Katharina Maloney from her e-mail
to the author on March 7, 2016, translated by Angelika Mendes-Lowney.

85 *appealed to everyday Catholics:* "Mother Angelica, 1923–2016," *National Catholic
Register,* March 28, 2016, accessed August 2, 2016, http://www.ncregister.com/dai-
ly-news/mother-angelica-1923-20161?.

86 *ninety-day implementation "sprint":* Jennifer Alsever, "Startups . . . Inside Giant
Companies," *Fortune,* May 1, 2016, 34.

87 *Change Without Pain:* Eric Abrahamson, "Change Without Pain," *Harvard Business
Review,* July–August, 2000, accessed August 2, 2016, https://hbr.org/2000/07/
change-without-pain/ar/1.

87 *Holy Venture Capital Funds and Holy Angel Investors:* Within the investment banking
industry, "venture capital" refers to investment funds committed to early stage
projects or companies. Similarly, "Angel Investors" place early-stage investments
in entrepreneurial ideas. Both approaches could be adapted to support fledgling
entrepreneurial ministries within the church.

90 *Elephants Can't Dance:* Louis V. Gerstner, *Who Says Elephants Can't Dance? Leading
a Great Enterprise through Dramatic Change* (New York: HarperBusiness: 2002),
First Edition.

91 *moral imagination:* Quotes from Matt Bannick, Jacqueline Novogratz, and Thane
Kreiner from discussions and email correspondence during Oct. and Nov. 2015.

93  *except those beliefs*: "A Business and Its Beliefs," *IBM website*, accessed August 2, 2016, http://www-03.ibm.com/ibm/history/ibm100/us/en/icons/bizbeliefs/.

94  *Spirit of the great explorers*: Joshua J. McElwee, "Catholicism Can and Must Change, Francis Forcefully Tells Italian Church Gathering," *National Catholic Reporter*, Nov. 10, 2015, accessed August 2, 2016, https://www.ncronline.org/news/vatican/catholi cism-can-and-must-change-francis-forcefully-tells-italian-church-gathering.

### Chapter 7: How Do You Know You're Successful? An Accountable Church

101  *money laundering, tax evasion*: Nick Squires, "Pope Francis: Will the Reforms of the 'Reform Pope' Stick," *The Christian Science Monitor*, Nov. 24, 2015, accessed August 2, 2016, http://www.csmonitor.com/World/Europe/2015/1124/Pope -Francis-Will-the-reforms-of-the-reform-pope-stick.

101  *know how to fix this*: All quotes with "Monica" from her discussion with the author on November 16, 2015.

103  *the duty to manifest*: CIC, Bk. II, Pt I, Title I, Can. 212, #3.

103  *glass house*: From a January 27, 1984, meeting of John Paul II with journalists, quoted in John Norton, "Traveling Companions: Journalists and Evangelists," *OSV News weekly*, Feb 24, 2008, accessed August 2, 2016, https://www.osv.com/OSVNews weekly/DailyTake/ConfessionsofaCatholicDad/Post/TabId/1831/ArtMID/17506/ ArticleID/9966/Traveling-companions-journalists-and-evangelists-.aspx.

103  *not fear transparency*: Francis, "Meeting with the Bishops of Mexico: Address of His Holiness Pope Francis," Feb 13, 2016, accessed August 2, 2016, https:// w2.vatican.va/content/francesco/en/speeches/2016/february/documents/ papa-francesco_20160213_messico-vescovi.html.

105  *Catholics rank way down*: Michael Paulson, "To Tithe or Not to Tithe . . . ," *New York Times*, Sunday Review, Jan 29, 2012, 7.

105  *transparent with its finances*: "Report of the Church in America: Leadership Roundtable 2004 at The Wharton School," July 9 and 10, 2004, 33, accessed Aug. 4, 2016, http://www.theleadershiproundtable.org/tlr/documents/Final perce nt20Report.pdf.

105  *natural disaster, and disease*: "Peter's Pence," *United States Conference of Catholic Bishops*, accessed August 2, 2016, http://www.usccb.org/catholic-giving/ opportunities-for-giving/peters-pence/.

106  *$8 billion annually:* John L. Allen, Jr., "The Church's Deep Pockets, the Butler Did It, and Myths about Atheism," *National Catholic Reporter*, Aug. 17, 2012, accessed August 2, 2016, http://ncronline.org/blogs/all-things-catholic/churchs-deep-pockets -butler-did-it-and-myths-about-atheism.

106  *Financial Times*: Frederick W. Gluck, "God's Line Manager," *Financial Times*, May 7, 2005, accessed August 2, 2016, http://www.ft.com/cms/s/0/282941fc-be95 -11d9-9473-00000e2511c8.html#axzz4DqwZM75n.

107  *single parish or a diocese*: Quotes from Fred Gluck from discussion with the author on Sept. 30, 2015.

108  *step by step*: Jim Collins, *Good to Great: Why Some Companies Make the Leap . . . and Others Don't* (New York: Harper Collins, 2001), 165, 174.

109  *We betrayed your trust*: James V. Johnston, Jr., "Homily for the Service of Lament," June 26, 2016, at Diocese of Kansas City-St. Joseph website, accessed August 2, 2016, https://kcsjcatholic.org/homily-for-service-of-lament/.

110  *same-sex attraction*: Timothy M. Dolan, "All Are Welcome," *CardinalDolan.org*, April 25, 2013, accessed August 2, 2016, http://cardinaldolan.org/index.php/all-are-welcome/.

111  *secret to quality is love*: Fitzhugh Mullan, "A Founder of Quality Assessment Encounters a Troubled System Firsthand," *Health Affairs*, accessed August 2, 2016, http://content.healthaffairs.org/content/20/1/137.long.

111  *creating better structures*: John Paul II, "Address of John Paul II to the Bishops of the Ecclesiastical Region of Pennsylvania and New Jersey (U.S.A) on Their 'Ad Limina' Visit," Sept. 11, 2004, accessed Oct. 16, 2016, https://w2.vatican.va/content/john-paul-ii/en/speeches/2004/september/documents/hf_jp-ii_spe_20040911_ad-limina-usa.html.

### Chapter 8: Wet Socks: A Church That Serves All in Need

113  *anything big-time*: This and all subsequent quotes from Sr. Rita Scully: discussion with the author on Oct. 15, 2015.

116  *toss the coin*: Francis, "Vigil of Pentecost with the Ecclesial Movements, Address of the Holy Father Francis," May 18, 2013, accessed August 2, 2016, https://w2.vatican.va/content/francesco/en/speeches/2013/may/documents/papa-francesco_20130518_veglia-pentecoste.html.

116  *see a poor man*: Quoted in Gary Anderson, "I Give, Therefore I Am—The Meaning of Charity in Jewish and Christian Thought," *Tikvah Center Working Paper*, #3, 2011, 10, accessed August 2, 2016, http://www.law.nyu.edu/sites/default/files/TikvahWorkingPapersArchive/WP3Anderson.pdf.

118  *cardinal's red hat*: Patrice Athanasidy, "Cardinal to Manhattan College Grads: Love God, Neighbor," *Catholic New York*, May 31, 2012, 17.

119  *no hands but yours*: Quotes from Sr. Simone, Hassan, and Fatma from transcript of interviews conducted by Ms. Petra Dankova in October 2015.

123  *American Catholics Today:* William V. D'Antonio, James D. Davidson, Dean R. Hoge, Mary L. Gautier, *American Catholics Today: New Realities of Their Faith and Their Church* (Lanham, MD: Rowman & Littlefield, 2007).

123  *Modern man listens: Evangelii Nuntiandi*, #41.

124  *their benevolence to strangers*: Julian the Apostate, "Letter to Arsacius, High-Priest of Galatia," in Wilmer Cave Wright, trans., *The Works of the Emperor Julian, III* (New York: G. P. Putnam's Sons, 1923).

124  *every one of these virtues*: Ibid.

124  *the Face of Christ*: Benedict XVI, "Opening of the Pastoral Convention of the Diocese of Rome on the Theme: 'Church Membership and Pastoral Co-Responsibility.' Address of His Holiness Benedict XVI," June 4, 2009, accessed August 2, 2016, https://zenit.org/articles/benedict-xvi-s-message-to-rome-conference-on-laity/.

124  *just order in society*: Benedict XVI, "Address of His Holiness Benedict XVI to Italian Christian Executives (U.C.I.D.)," March 4, 2006, accessed August 2, 2016,

http://w2.vatican.va/content/benedict-xvi/en/speeches/2006/march/documents/
hf_ben-xvi_spe_20060304_ucid.html.

125 *Yes, ma'am it is*: *Sacred Stories*, Fifteenth Edition, (Denver: Catholic Health Initiatives), 8–10, accessed August 2, 2016, http://www.catholichealthinitiatives.org/
sacred-stories-archive.

### Chapter 9: The Glow: A Church That Transforms Hearts and Souls

127 *Some 13 percent former Catholics*: The exact figure is 12.9 percent, from: "America's
Changing Religious Landscape," Pew Research Center.

127 *more than 8 million people*: The Pew Research "Faith in Flux" survey found that
5 percent of adult Americans are former Catholics who now worship at Protestant churches, 71 percent of these because their spiritual needs were not met
as Catholics, accessed August 2, 2016, http://www.pewforum.org/2009/04/27/
faith-in-flux/. I calculated 8 million by applying these percentage figures against
the 2013 US census bureau estimate of 242 million US adults, accessed August
2, 2016, https://www.reference.com/government-politics/many-adults-live-usa-
b830ecdfb6047660.

130 *God cannot exist*: All quotes from a discussion with the author, date withheld at
request of "Beatrice."

133 *the faith, the freedom*: Ad Gentes

133 *rejoice at goodness*: Benedict XVI, "Meeting with the Young People of Sardinia,
Address of His Holiness Benedict XVI," Sept 7, 2008, accessed August 2, 2016,
http://w2.vatican.va/content/benedict-xvi/en/speeches/2008/september/docu-
ments/hf_ben-xvi_spe_20080907_cagliari-giovani.pdf.

135 *changing their lives*: This and all subsequent quotes from Greg Hawkins from a
discussion with the author, November 3, 2015.

137 *Move*: Greg L. Hawkins and Cally Parkinson, *Move: What 1,000 Churches Reveal
about Spiritual Growth* (Grand Rapids, MI: Zondervan, 2011), First Ed.

140 *tough choices and new sacrifices*: Blaise Cupich, "'Renew My Church': Dreaming Big
about the Archdiocese of Chicago," *Catholic New World*, Feb. 7–20, 2016, accessed
August 2, 2016, http://www.catholicnewworld.com/column/archbishop-cupich/
2016/02/07/renew-my-church.

141 *pastoral responsibility: Catechism*, #879.

### Chapter 10: Dusty Shoes: A Church That Reaches Out to Engage the World

143 *ten thousand places*: Gerard Manley Hopkins, S. J., "As Kingfishers Catch Fire," in
Norman H. Mackenzie, ed. *The Poetical Works of Gerard Manley Hopkins* (Oxford:
Clarendon Press, 1990), 141.

149 *kind and generous*: Augustine, *Confesssions*, Book V, #13, in J. G. Pilkington,
trans., *Nicene and Post-Nicene Fathers, First Series*, Vol. 1., ed. Philip Schaff
(Buffalo, NY: Christian Literature Publishing Co., 1887.), revised and edited for
New Advent by Kevin Knight, accessed August 2, 2016, http://www.newadvent.
org/fathers/110105.htm.

150 *solemn nonsense*: Michael Sean Winters, "Pope Francis' Latest Bombshell Interview," *National Catholic Reporter*, Oct 1, 2013, accessed August 2, 2016, https://

www.ncronline.org/blogs/distinctly-catholic/pope-francis-latest-bombshell
-interview.

150  *engage in proselytism*: Benedict XVI, "Holy Mass for the Inauguration of the Fifth
General Conference of the Bishops of Latin America and the Caribbean, Homily
of His Holiness Benedict XVI," May 13, 2007, accessed August 2, 2016, http://
w2.vatican.va/content/benedict-xvi/en/homilies/2007/documents/hf_ben-xvi
_hom_20070513_conference-brazil.html.

150  *someone invited me*: "Faith in Flux," *Pew Research Center*, April 27, 2009 (revised
Feb. 2011), 29, accessed October 16, 2016, http://www.pewforum.org/2009/04/27/
faith-in-flux/.

150  *87 percent of Protestant megachurch*: Scott Thumma and Warren Bird, "Not Who
You Think They Are: A Profile of the People Who Attend America's Mega-
churches," *Hartford Institute for Religion Research*, June 9, 2009, accessed August 2,
2016, http://hirr.hartsem.edu/megachurch/megachurch_attender_report.htm.

151  *lopsided ratio of losses*: "America's Changing Religious Landscape: Christians
Decline Sharply as Share of Population; Unaffiliated and Other Faiths Continue
to Grow," *Pew Research Center: Religion & Public Life*, May 12, 2015, accessed
August 2, 2016, http://www.pewforum.org/2015/05/12/americas-changing-reli-
gious-landscape/.

151  *doors of our churches*: Carol Glatz, "God Never Shuts the Door; Church Always
Must Be Open, Too, Pope Says," *Catholic News Service*, Nov 18, 2015, accessed
August 2, 2016, http://www.catholicnews.com/services/englishnews/2015/pope
-says-god-never-shuts-the-door.cfm.

152  *walking at people's side*: Francis, "Apostolic Journey to Rio De Janeiro on the
Occasion of the XXVIII World Youth Day. Meeting with the Bishops of Brazil:
Address of Pope Francis," July 28, 2013, accessed August 2, 2016, https://w2.vati-
can.va/content/francesco/en/speeches/2013/july/documents/papa
-francesco_20130727_gmg-episcopato-brasile.html.

152  *stale air of closed rooms*: Francis, "Pope: Mission, the Best Cure for the Church,"
April 18, 2013, accessed August 2, 2016, http://en.radiovaticana.va/storico/
2013/04/18/pope_mission,_the_best_cure_for_the_church/en1-683985.

152  *who need help most*: Thomas C. Fox, "Francis Speaks of Church Harmony, Service
to the Poor," *National Catholic Reporter*, May 19, 2013, accessed August 2, 2016,
http://ncronline.org/blogs/ncr-today/francis-speaks-church-harmony-service-poor.

154  *culture of encounter* : Francis, "Vigil of Pentecost with the Ecclesial Movements,
Address of the Holy Father Francis," May 18, 2013, accessed August 2, 2016,
https://w2.vatican.va/content/francesco/en/speeches/2013/may/documents/papa
-francesco_20130518_veglia-pentecoste.html.

156  *by the age of twenty-three*: John L. Allen, Jr., "In America's Religious Marketplace,
the Real Catholic Problem Is New Sales," *National Catholic Reporter*, Feb. 11,
2011, accessed August 2, 2016, https://www.ncronline.org/blogs/all-things-catho-
lic/americas-religious-marketplace-real-catholic-problem-new-sales.

157  *Nigeria's Maiduguri*: Carey Lodge, "Nigeria: At Least 5,000 Catholics Killed by
Boko Haram," *Christian Today*, May 13, 2015, accessed August 2, 2016, http://

www.christiantoday.com/article/nigeria.at.least.5000.catholics.killed.by.boko .haram/53864.htm.

157 *more martyrs in the Church*: "Pope: There Are More Christian Martyrs Today Than Ever," June 30, 2014, accessed August 2, 2016, http://en.radiovaticana.va/news/ 2014/06/30/pope_there_are_more_christian_martyrs_today_than_ever/1102363.

158 *multiply wells where thirsting*: "Synodus Episcoporum Bulletin, XIII Ordinary General Assembly of the Synod of Bishops. 7-28 October, 2012," #30, Oct. 26, 2012, accessed August 2, 2016, http://www.vatican.va/news_services/press/sinodo/ documents/bollettino_25_xiii-ordinaria-2012/02_inglese/b30_02.html.

159 *never abandon them*: Evangelii Gaudium, #48.

*Chapter 11: Jolted from Tiredness: The Holy Spirit Has Placed Us on the Playing Field*

161 *the effectiveness of the church* This and following quotes from Archbishop Gerald Kicanas, from Nov 1, 2006 "The Future of Catholic Parish Ministry," The Church in the 21st Century Center, Boston College, accessed August 2, 2016, http://www .bc.edu/church21/webcast.html?kicanas256K_Stream.mp4#feature-area.

161 *decrease by a third*: Archbishop Kicanas attributed the statistic to: William V. D'Antonio, James D. Davidson, Dean R. Hoge, Mary L. Gautier, *American Catholics Today: New Realities of Their Faith and Their Church* (Lanham, MD: Rowman & Littlefield, 2007).

161 *old solutions to new problems:* "The Transformation Mandate: Leadership Imperatives for a Hyperconnected World," *Heidrick & Struggles*, 2016, 48, accessed August 2, 2016, http://www.heidrick.com/~/media/Publications percent20and percent20Reports/The-Transformation-Mandate.pdf.

163 *crisis of today*: This and other quotes in this paragraph from: Joseph Ratzinger, *Faith and the Future*, trans. from the German original published in 1970 as *Glaube und Zukunft* (Chicago: Franciscan Herald Press, 1971), 103–105.

165 *initiative of its individual*: Faith and the Future, 103–105.

165 *how far we can go*: Inés San Martín, "Trusted Papal Aide Says Woman Could be Vatican's Prime Minister," *Crux*, May 4, 2016, accessed August 2, 2016, https:// cruxnow.com/church/2016/05/04/trusted-papal-aide-says-woman-could-be -vaticans-prime-minister/.

167 *in all things, charity* John XXIII, "*Ad Petri Cathedram* Encyclical of Pope John XXIII on Truth, Unity and Peace, In a Spirit of Charity," June 29, 1959, #72, accessed August 2, 2016, http://w2.vatican.va/content/john-xxiii/en/encyclicals/ documents/hf_j-xxiii_enc_29061959_ad-petri.html.

168 *the way out of the grave*: G. K. Chesterton, *The Everlasting Man* (Tacoma, WA: Angelico Press, 2013).

168 *being how they were before*: Francis, "Priests to Face Epoch Change as a Challenge to Seek Out the Remote," *Vatican Information Service*, Sept. 16, 2013, accessed August 2, 2016, http://www.news.va/en/news/priests-to-face-epoch-change-as-a-challenge-to-see·

169 *opportunity for leadership*: Peter F. Drucker, *Managing in Turbulent Times* (New York: Harper & Row, 1980), 5.

# INDEX